RICHARD WHITFIELD

MASTERING
E-MOTIONS

FEELING OUR WAY INTELLIGENTLY IN RELATIONSHIP

Copyright © 2005 O Books
O Books is an imprint of John Hunt Publishing Ltd., The Bothy,
Deershot Lodge, Park Lane, Ropley, Hants, SO24 0BE, UK
office@johnhunt-publishing.com
www.O-books.net

Distribution in:
UK
Orca Book Services
orders@orcabookservices.co.uk
Tel: 01202 665432 Fax: 01202 666219 Int. code (44)

USA and Canada
NBN
custserv@nbnbooks.com
Tel: 1 800 462 6420 Fax: 1 800 338 4550

Australia
Brumby Books
sales@brumbybooks.com
Tel: 61 3 9761 5535 Fax: 61 3 9761 7095

New Zealand
Peaceful Living
books@peaceful-living.co.nz
Tel: 64 09 921 6222 Fax: 64 09 921 6220

Singapore
STP
davidbuckland@tlp.com.sg
Tel: 65 6276 Fax: 65 6276 7119

South Africa
Alternative Books
altbook@global.co.za
Tel: 27 011 792 7730 Fax: 27 011 972 7787

Text: © Richard Whitfield 2005

Design: BookDesign™, London, UK

ISBN 1 905047 26 6

A CIP catalogue record for this book is available from the
British Library.

Printed in the USA by Maple-Vail Manufacturing Group

RICHARD WHITFIELD

MASTERING E-MOTIONS

FEELING OUR WAY INTELLIGENTLY IN RELATIONSHIP

BOOKS

WINCHESTER UK
NEW YORK USA

REVIEWS

This perceptive and enlightened book, written by a widely experienced and research-informed teacher, provides fine insights and know-how for improved personal emotional management.
Professor Windy Dryden, Counselling Psychologist, University of London Goldsmiths College

An unusual, informed and creative synthesis that will help many readers to gain insights into their capricious feelings, and hence personalities, values and belief systems, promoting deeper reflection and wiser action.
Professor John Friesen, Professor Emeritus, Department of Counselling Psychology, University of British Columbia and formerly Head of Counselling and Psychological Services, Department of Education, Government of Alberta, Canada

This bold, challenging and practical book should prompt responses in lifestyle and outlook. Although aiding the individual, the text helps awaken our collective democratic consciousness to the massive evolutionary risks that we face unless we mind and master our emotions.
Margaret Austin, Educator, former New Zealand Cabinet Minister for Science and Arts, now Chair of the NZ National Commission for UNESCO

In an age of widespread mistrust, when the problematic glue of society is a mix of political correctness and procedural detail that inhibit an individual's growth into wholeness, this book comes as a tonic. It gets to the heart of a basic 'Golden Rule' Christian principle, the practical nature of love, and the loving of both neighbour and self that have the power to transform. This text is a must for those seeking to minister to others at any level.
David Bick, pastoral counsellor, spiritual director, author and Anglican priest

The quality of relational and emotional climates of home and school shape the foundations for optimum learning. Here is vital, practical guidance for parents, teachers and carers who desire to become more literate emotionally, thereby enhancing their own and others' lives.
David Williams, Headmaster of Kinross-Wolaroi School, New South Wales, Australia

A refreshing approach to basic emotional and relational literacy, now so widely needed amid extensive relational turmoil and its often devastating impacts on couples, family life, community and workplace.
Professor David Olson, President of Life Innovations, originator of the PREPARE/ENRICH programme for couples, formerly Professor of Family Social Science, University of Minnesota

DEDICATION

For Shirley, a friend since childhood, tenacious wife since 1961
and fine mother from 1965

Related works by Richard Whitfield

Education for Family Life, Hodder and Stoughton, 1980

Families Matter (ed), Marshall Pickering, 1986

Learning to Love, National Family Trust, 1990

Life Foundations (Leader Guides/Student Journals),

NES Arnold, 1992-3

Foundations for a Good Life, (Leader Guide/Student Journal),

Marriage Care, 2001

Young People as Citizens Now, Youth Work Press, 1997

Taproots for Transformation: Discernment in an Irrational World,
A Dialogue with Bishop Bruce Gilberd, Shannon Press SA, 2005

A trilogy concerning life shape, illustrated poetically, published by
Bracken Bank Books:

Transformations: A Spiritual Memoir, 2000

Purpose in Presence: Cameos on Attachment and Social Action, 2001

Messages in Time: Life Path and Love's Pattern, 2002

Also:

Lifelines: Poems for Pocket or Pillow, Bracken Bank Books, 2004

ACKNOWLEDGEMENTS

I am grateful to various audiences of young and old around the world upon whom I have tested the core ideas here presented over the past 20 years.

Several friends have shown patient and active listening, so helping me, over some three decades, to steer variously through patches of emotional, relational and spiritual fog for which I might have been better prepared. In particular I thank: *David Bick* (Anglican priest, counsellor-tutor and author); *John Bradshaw*, psychologist, counsellor and colleague (1975-82); *Ann Jenkins-Hansen*, Health Visitor and founder of the New Parent-Infant Network; *Raymond O'Malley* (1912-1997), English specialist and Cambridge University colleague, 1966-75 (who once, memorably, said to me that he would not seek a friend who was not capable of falling in love); and *Brian Tebbut*, counsellor, pastoral group tutor and Methodist Minister.

The manuscript passed in draft, at different stages, through the hands of my son-in-law Keith Stewart, eldest son Mark, and my wife Shirley, each of whom made helpful comments and gave encouragement for which I am grateful. I also wish to express my gratitude to several variously distinguished colleagues around the globe who have graciously commended this book, and to John Hunt who had faith in becoming the publisher and helped sharpen some of my focus.

PREFACE

Almost every human thought and action has emotional underpinnings. Human feelings and emotions are the gateway to the intellect and the essence of inner spirit.

This book offers readers insight and guidance for the management and mastery of their feelings and emotions so as to enhance self-understanding and the quality of personal relationships. The material drawn together here has massive implications for our personal and social priorities, and for those in positions of political, social and educational leadership, if we dare be rational about social sustainability.

Awareness and internal monitoring of our individual and collective emotions is a form of 'management' that is largely unseen, but has immense impacts upon us individually, and in our relationships, including our participation in human organisations. Most of us can grow in emotional management without specific therapeutic help, through reading, structured discussion with friends, and self-help exercises. Sadly, so far at least, mainstream education does little within this important field, so crucial for cultural well-being.

The text is based upon my practical interpretation for 'ordinary life' of a diverse but often inaccessible background literature, along with my own remedial experience as a sometime 'emotional illiterate'. Keeping technical jargon to a minimum, the book is intended for a wide readership, male and female, professional and lay, those of religious faith or none, and for all within or beyond adolescence. Students of 'management' will also profit from the text.

The overall goal of *enhancing emotional literacy and personal relational sensitivity* may be summarised by four more specific *aims*:

1. To promote understanding of the interconnections between human thinking, personal experience, feelings and actions, so as to sensitise the 'intelligence of feeling', and thereby enhancing the ability to feel intelligently.

2. To enrich language and communication skills concerning feelings and emotions.

3. To enhance the safe management of emotions in a range of relational situations.

4. To introduce connections between emotional being, personal identity and 'spiritual life' so as to help enhance personal contentment, even happiness.

My hope is that the book will be welcomed as an accessible contribution to the growth of emotional awareness within the general population. It can also support the work of teachers, counsellors, medical personnel, pastors and friends who endeavour to help others in the many-sided and universal phenomenon of emotional distress.

The style of *Mastering Emotions* is unthreatening, and illustrated by examples within a framework of sensitive ethics. In application it will extend relational capability in a range of contexts, including home and family, and within workplace and community. Readers can thereby be spared costly anguish, and enhance their general health and wellness.

Optional personal exercises appear at relevant points within the text. These are designed to prompt individual reflection and to build up inner confidence concerning emotional management. While these activities may suggest issues for discussion with perhaps one or two trusted others, the commended 'personal notebook' exercise record is in principle intended to be confidential (see note on page 13).

The select bibliography (page 262) reflects some of the strands of thought that have influenced elements in this particular synthesis.

Feedback on this book, or requests for related lectures and seminars, should be via e-mail to: rw@richardwhitfield.co.uk (website: www.richardwhitfield.co.uk) and/or telephone: (UK) 01297-442529

Richard Whitfield,
Bracken Bank,
Timber Hill,
Lyme Regis,
Dorset, DT7 3HQ, UK
June 2005

CONTENTS

1

FEELING INTELLIGENTLY IN OUR EMOTIONAL LANDSCAPE

FEELING INTELLIGENTLY IN OUR EMOTIONAL LANDSCAPE

*'Each of us makes our own weather, determines the colour
of the skies in the emotional universe which each inhabits.'*
Fulton Sheen, 1895-1979, in *Way to Happiness*

1.1 The emotional mind

With well over a century of the provision of universal education in Western societies, and masses of people now studying to become smartly qualified – supposedly using their minds to good effect – within thousands of universities and colleges, it is surprising that, for all the improvements in material provision and public health, alongside the wonders of modern science and technology, there remains so much emotional and relational turmoil, and a lack of inner settlement, contentment and peace. Have we been seduced to believe that our species, somewhat arrogantly labeled long ago as *homo sapiens*, has become just that, 'wise man'?

For all around us, and sometimes within us, we still see our kith and kin, and nations, acting crazily in relation to both their short and long-term interests. Eating, drinking and drug-taking habits, disrespect for the psychological security of infants and children, varieties of breakdown of family relationships, driving motor vehicles without due care and attention, the waging of dubious wars, and too many young men committing suicide are but a few examples. The so-called 'smart' mind is in fact often waylaid by un-smart and often impetuous emotions.

The scientific reality is that our feelings and emotions underpin *all* our thoughts and actions. This is true even for highly trained airline pilots and traffic controllers, failures in their complex kit accounting for less than ten per cent of civil air accidents. 'Human error' in situations of potential stress is more often emotional than intellectual. Consequently we are a doomed species, our own worst enemy, destined to act against our individual and collective best interests, unless we all seriously 'wise up' on our feelings and emotions. Far more than our rational intellects, feelings and emotions govern every important aspect of life, the choices we make, and the risks we do or don't take.

Emotional factors greatly influence our educational and work performance, our friendships, our voting and spending patterns, our life and career choices, our sexual and family lives, and, not least, our ethical and religious dispositions. Yet our culture, only wedded narrowly and superficially to reason, offers little that helps us to bridge gaps between our emotions and the good reasoning that could achieve much improved personal contentment, and also, crucially, interpersonal harmony in family life, classrooms, workplaces, and on national and international stages. Our natural longings for peace, and freedom from emotional pain, must in reality begin from within each inner life, whatever the range of predisposing circumstances, many of which are far from perfect.

To take an extreme case, terrorism is not mainly about territory, but more to do with often partly justified anger (an innate emotion) concerning perceived injustices, pressed to become way beyond any moral and physical control. Some people land themselves in prison because, under stress, they lost emotional control, perhaps delivering impetuous kicks or punches that they later regretted, and whose angry origins they barely understood. Similar examples of emotional fog, including depressed moods and everyday anxieties, drug abuse and sexual promiscuity, litter the wreckage of many family lives, professional and business concerns.

So long as we lack emotional expertise, getting heart and head into better unison, through which emerges both preventative tactics and the latent healing of prior wounds, we will, in a world of awesome choices, continue to destroy much of what can be great in life.

This book addresses these important issues conceptually and practically, using a fresh, research-informed, yet basically uncomplicated approach to emotional literacy. Involved are insights that enhance the deep compassion and consideration for oneself and others, that much neglected age-old 'golden-rule' wisdom.

However, these often-elusive golden-rule qualities of respecting and our loving neighbor and ourselves must be both learned, and handed on by experience, for although they are our longing, they are far from being innate at birth. This learning and handing on has always been far from perfect, but we are now much more aware of the actions and environments that can aid our optimum human development from womb to tomb. That we act upon that kind of knowledge far too infrequently in personal and collective choices at home, in employment, in community organization and, not least, national politics, is the greatest irrationality of we modern people. If the neglect of emotional and spiritual awareness within real-time decision making is perpetuated in our culture of high expectations, we, for sure, endanger our safe planetary existence, with unimaginable consequences and suffering.

1.1 Some probing questions

In primary school, you and I learned a lot about the famed *three 'R's*, reading, writing and arithmetic, but little explicitly about the *fourth R* of human and other relationships, within which is entwined whatever emotional know-how we may have gleaned. So now toy for a few moments with these key, personal questions.

Do you think you are emotionally literate? By this I mean several things, principally matters of language use, inner comfortableness, and appropriate personal control of the emotional arena that you know exists inside you, which sometimes messes up aspects of your own and maybe other people's lives. This can happen at home, at work and even sometimes in leisure pursuits like competitive games, which often have a great deal of emotional content.

So further questions arise, such as:

- Do you have a good or a fuzzy grip on the various words that we use for our feelings and emotions? How many emotions do you think you have? And how many feelings? Do you use those two words interchangeably?

- Do you think emotions are innate at birth, or are they learned later? Or, are only some inborn and others learned through our social experience?

- Do some of your emotions, or other people's emotional reactions towards you, trouble you? For example, do you tend to equate anger with personal dislike?

- Do you ever feel embarrassed or slightly threatened? If so what sort of things cause or have caused these feelings?

- When you look in the mirror, you can see your body, perhaps all of it with the aid of more than one mirror. However, the same does not quite apply to your emotions. Which emotions do you think you hide most, from yourself and from other people? What are the consequences of such cover-ups?

- Have you any particular feelings and emotions in relation to your body? Do these make any difference to the ways you dress and behave?

- If you have any particular enemies, how do you tend to feel about and act towards such people?

- Have you considered if sometimes you may attribute or 'project' your own repressed inner feelings and motives onto others, perceiving them as you dare not yourself?

- How do you feel about being born, and about, one day, dying?

I do not expect you to answer all these questions easily right now, but when you have read the book, and maybe done the reflective exercises suggested within the chapters, you might return to them. There will be a late reminder!

We can all learn to manage our emotions, just like we can learn to exercise our bodies. But most of us have never have been taught how to do this. They don't teach it to us at school, and, later, only to a few for specialist therapeutic use. It's taken me too much of a lifetime to learn how to do it, even though I've been seen as something of a so-called expert on the subject for some of that time. As my wife knows best, I can on occasion still get in an emotional tangle, but I handle the issues rather better than I used to. This is why I think what I have to say might help you. I know what the experts say, and even though nobody has complete mastery of their emotional states, what is known is based upon sound scholarship, though this is often buried in technical language in literature that is remote from the everyday.

So here I have done my best to address the sorts of questions posed above, to distil insights and experience so as to help readers take a few shortcuts towards better emotional awareness and management. The results can include a better sense of comfort of being in your own shoes, and less discomfort in a range of human interactions that combine to form the living fabric of your relationships. These relationships, as we will see in chapter 2, are not only with other people, but also specific objects, the biophysical environment, and even a sense of comfort and friendliness with 'God' if you dare to consider such a creative power or being, spelt with those three letters or otherwise.

Of course nobody can possibly get through life without some experience of emotional trauma, such as a car accident, losing one's job, moving home and neighborhood, or the death of a loved one. However this book will I hope help you to navigate around some of the rocks that tend to be unseen during emotional high tides!

1.2 Emotions and life outlook

Our emotions profoundly affect our outlook on life, and in particular the development and maintenance of both our self-esteem and our relationships. If we are to lead reasonably fulfilled lives as relational and social beings, we need both to understand and to manage our emotions. As we will see, this is a practical matter requiring more inner reflection than most of us are accustomed to, yet still harmonizing with our fundamental essence and zest.

Friends, colleagues and relatives, not least spouses, are bequeathed 'for better and for worse' with their own and others' prior emotional perceptions and experiences. These form sometimes deeply hidden 'stories', aspects of which are not generally stored in the surface layers of consciousness. Sometimes the distressful feelings experienced at the time (including babyhood, before the acquisition of language) were so painful that the experience became effectively deleted or suppressed from conscious memory. The good enough management of important relationships is aided when perceptions are sensitized, emotional awareness and literacy are enlarged, and, within a context of trust and safety, personal stories relevant to self and other understanding are told, enabling the release of more genuine love and compassion. Those precious commodities are what make our human 'world go round'. Learning how to enrich such possibilities is the underlying purpose of this book.

Our emotions need to be mastered, and therefore to be 'minded', that is, reasonably engaged with our intellects so that we can 'feel intelligently'. Dissociations – 'splits' between our 'head and heart' – tend to prompt incoherence and unpredictability in our lives, sometimes with severe consequences, such as losing our jobs, messing up our marriages or other important relationships, or, at the extreme, even going to prison. Certainly, anyone's life is enhanced if they can achieve and manage a reasonable unison between considered thoughts and feelings. If our emotions develop a life of their own they can get us into all sorts of trouble, unaligned with our own best interests.

Emotions are inherently relational, and the gaps within our human interfacing are stunningly varied. They include gaps in the circuitry and component layout of our amazing brains, between our intellects and feelings (our head and heart tussles), and gaps within gender, age, perceptions, values, behavior and 'faith'. Furthermore, most of us are unprepared for negotiating the taxing gaps, conflicts, paradoxes and perplexities that we encounter in the partly predictable phases and stages of everyday life.

Personnel management, now often known as 'human resource' management, is an important branch of Management Studies. Fancy titles notwithstanding, this has always been the preoccupation of those having responsibility for staff at work, but, far more pervasively, as people caring for others in the everyday of home and community life. Such 'people management', whether in employment or at home, or in the community, tends to go awry if our perceptions and procedural actions are insensitive, immature, 'brain-unfriendly' and thereby sensed as emotionally hostile. Indeed, our perceptions of another's integrity can be bound up as much with the ways in which they come over emotionally as whether they tell the truth.

Our hidden, inner emotional management, or lack of it, actually impacts upon almost everything that we engage in. Sadly, in our culture, we get little or no help with this crucial form of management. A minority of us braves the consulting room to see a therapist or counselor, almost always because of some obvious crisis involving clear emotional pain and turmoil. Such settings are of a remedial nature, aiming to fix or redesign broken parts, rather than the wiser preventative attention that is the main focus here. Often it is extraordinarily difficult for us to perceive and to learn new insights and skills when we are emotionally upset. Prevention of likely foreseeable problems is ever better than cure of avoidable pain.

1.4 Gaping gaps: owning up to emotional mismanagement.

Human feelings, which cannot be physically touched, though they may be physically triggered, are as real as atoms, apples and anchors. No less than minding the gap between train and platform, we twenty-first century people must learn to watch, mind and bridge the gaps in our emoting consciousness. Future world history depends probably more upon our feelings and emotions today than upon the pure reason of our intellects.

As we have noted, and further explained in chapters 2 and 3, we are first a feeling and relating species, not a fully logical and rational one. In fact, the development of rationality, or plain good sense depends first and foremost upon our emotional safety and well-being. Feelings and emotions are with us all the time, sometimes without conscious knowledge (as in newborn babies), and even in our strong and weak dreams while we are asleep.

Hence there are only two fundamental traits of mind, *feeling* and *willing*. The latter does involve the conscious mind and is about making plans to be or to act in particular ways, to make responses to the social and physical environment. Hence, *willing* is close to action management. So *emotional* management is about bringing *feeling* and *willing* close together, or bringing heart and head into a reasonable unison, the gap between them becoming variously bridged. Emotional *mis*management arises when heart and head are poorly synchronized. Then, action falls down in the un-minded gap between the two, often with harmful consequences. Sometimes it is hard for us to own up to such all too common inner-life mismanagement, let alone to make reparation.

Since, in the words of the present Poet Laureate, Andrew Motion, 'poetry is a hotline to the emotions', here posed are questions in poetic form that echo some of those encountered in section 1.2. But, as you read these few stanzas, try not to perceive them simply as a list of detailed emotional difficulties but rather as normalities in life, to be faced with a sense of hopefulness.

Emotional has-beens?

Have you ever ....
Known of your jumbled emotions
Aiding avoidable commotions
For both self and others,
Including sisters and brothers?
Or perceived a good life elusive
Through mixed feelings abusive?
Or been daunted by tangles of feeling
With mind boiling close to the ceiling?
                    If so, then read on!

Have you ever...
Kicked the cat,
Whacked the dog?
Been harsh with parents or kids,
Blown off futile lids,
Prompted strife in the house,
Or lashed out at your spouse?
Or been with workmates defensive,
And with neighbors offensive?
                    If so, then read on!

Have you ever lost your inner plot's best,
Even fouled inside your own nest?
Or felt your self wobble around,
Your feet barely touching the ground?
Or have vain hopes become somehow stuck
In repetitive, ghastly emotional muck?

Or are your sorrows so heavy,
Leeching too long a levy?
Or has your heart apart been torn
By some emotional or ethical storm?
Whether such became visible or not,
Inner disturbance is a life-draining rot.
                              So read on!

For this book may just help you
To sort out a baffling stew
Of your capricious emotions,
So you may have fewer commotions
Around your uniquely precious life,
As you learn to taper some strife,
To be more of a self-other blessing,
The good and godly life caressing.

So why hang, unsure of your strap,
When you can mind, then bridge the gap
Between head and heart?
Then play a more tuneful part
In this awesome Universe,
Become more a blessing than hazard or curse!

1.5 Emotions, relationships and the flow of this book

Most of the besetting human problems in this world are caused through ignorance of ourselves as emotional and spiritual creatures in relationship. Neither materialism nor science and technology are able to provide relaxed solutions to problems of living that arise from a lack of awareness of or respect for our emotional character. Upset emotions contribute significantly to car and other traffic accidents, to addictions and mental illness, to learning difficulties, to destructive arguments, to family breakdown, to political fortunes, to violence and moral deviation, and much else. It is in all our interests for us to learn about avenues through which our emotions might be managed to our own and society's benefit. We can then be, consistently, something other than our own worst enemy.

Here is an example, in her own words, of a 12-year-old girl who expresses a feeling of being ashamed of her lack of emotional control in an unexceptional family situation:

> 'I love my brother and sister, but when they annoy me, or don't get ready for school, which is going to make me and my Dad and brother late, I get angry with them and sometimes hurt them. I hate it; I feel really bad, and I would just like to be able to talk about it. But I don't think they really understand how I feel.'

This 'little' difficulty, serious business for the participants, is clearly unlikely to become resolved by the girl in isolation. The emotions here, as elsewhere, arise in a social context. Hence a collaborative opportunity is required, alongside language and related communication skills, in addition to a change in behavior, so as to achieve a better relational and feelings outcome. This girl's rather mature and reflective solution gets part of the way towards this:

> 'They need to stop trying to have fun all the time, and think about getting ready and doing what they are supposed to do; that is, be more considerate of me and Dad. I need to control my temper, and to talk to them calmly about all this without winding them up.'

Learning how to behave considerately, however, is often a complex undertaking. It involves 'getting into another person's shoes', a transition made more difficult if we have not had solid experience of others' felt consideration towards us. Consideration for others, an element of behaving lovingly, is not inborn but experienced first as a gift from others.

Emotional awareness and management are essentially practical matters, albeit illuminated by a framework of practical theory, as we will see. Following next is a first, simple *personal exercise*. It is likely that you will get much more out of this text, including deepened self-knowledge, if you have a shot at most, if not all, of the optional exercises.

Note of guidance about personal exercises suggested in this book:

All that is needed for each of the optional *personal exercises* in this book is a handy notebook of about A5 page size, pen or pencil, and, crucially, peace and quiet for no less than 20 to 30 minutes at a time. A small amount of writing is usually called for, advisedly with good spacing to allow for possible later additions. The written 'journal' notes that you make are confidential to you, though you may choose, later, to share parts of your inner reflections and 'enquiries' with a trusted and sensitive friend. Such a friend will be someone whom you feel is a good listener who does not make instant or rigid judgments, nor tries to dominate let alone take over even a part of your life.

Personal exercise I

Make a note concerning a recent incident at home, at work, or in some community activity, in which you believe you did not manage your feelings and emotions very well (whether just inside yourself, or visible to others, or both). Then note how you would have preferred to act in that situation, and also note anything that you might now do to make some reparation or to achieve more sense of inner comfort and equanimity.

Emotions, no less than intellect, are of the essence of our being. Interestingly, brain research is in important ways showing that our emotions tend to drive the intellect, rather than the other way round, as has been implicit in traditional theories of learning (see chapter 3). So emotions are set to move much more obviously centre-stage in this new millennium. Learning to 'mind', rather than being unconsciously manipulated by our emotions, is real cost-saving agenda!

Emotions are also related to what many traditions believe are the immortal aspects of the human spirit. Hence emotions must somehow become actively enfolded within any seriously defensible religious or spiritual life. In many westernized societies, the dominant religious movement that cradled so much of modernity, namely Christianity, has often been both suffocated and divided by over-polarized intellectual arguments. Yet intense emotional undercurrents generally accompany doctrinal disagreements. Often these reveal emotions associated with individuals' underlying insecurities, and quests for status, power and control, that many would see as barely compatible with the life and witness of Jesus.

What all of us need to recognize, is that emotions are not peripheral to the human quest for meaning. Indeed, quarrying truth in any field is always partly an emotional enterprise, even for scientists. To be strongly motivated towards any project or endeavor is to have invested emotional capital and energy in it. Therefore strong feelings and passions as to progress and outcome become inevitable.

Belatedly we are now becoming more aware that emotional competence and skills are essential to the good-enough conduct of our relational lives at all levels. Of course emotions always have been central in human welfare and behavior. The new development is that masses of us now hope for, and expect, almost as a right, relational satisfactions that our forebears regarded as a luxury beyond the frequently harsh realities of everyday toil for basic life provisions. Such higher expectations can be a rich life-enhancer, provided there is realism, and a sharing of concerns with insight and understanding.

Emotional enrichment can only rarely be an individualistic and private issue. More fundamentally it is a social activity, necessarily set within a framework of mutuality, and therefore respectful morality and a sense of fairness. This was clearly understood by the girl in the example given earlier. Without some preparedness for mutuality, the consequent self-centered emotional search for 'highs' of experience, for respect or for healing, almost always proves to be barren, and, at worst, exploitive of others.

The following is a summary of the broad directional flow of this book, giving the main issues covered in each chapter.

1. We need to understand that we are emotional and relational beings. We bring to all our relationships some emotional agenda. Moreover such agenda is not random. The mode and intensity with which we experience our emotions depends upon many factors, including biography, nurture, values and belief systems (chapter 2).

2. Our emotionality is set within the context of common phases of human development from conception. Brain sciences now greatly illuminate the dynamic complexities of human character and behavior (chapter 3).

3. It is both possible and desirable to map the key features of our emotional life, and to develop some common language surrounding this (chapter 4).

4. Everyone, across the globe, has the same basic emotions. Some of these, about six in number, are innate at birth (chapter 5). Love, though not our longing for it, is perhaps paradoxically not one of these innate emotions. Neither is guilt, nor its related sense of shame, these being better described as 'learned emotions' (chapter 6). Love that is reliable, rather than of a fleeting romantic or sexual kind, is viewed as a gift of commitment from another to be actively received, rather than a discreet emotion to be managed (chapter 7).

5. Some important gender differences are apparent in emotional management and outlook; some of these being culturally related. These differences overlay a great deal of emotional commonality between the sexes. Such differences can be unhelpfully exaggerated, and nobody benefits from falsely polarized 'gender wars' (chapter 8).

6. It is possible, but not easy, for us to manage human emotional life, rather than to experience it as merely happening 'in our face', like an unpredictable outpouring from a waterfall. Lifestyle conditions for the active management of our emotions include commitments to seeking insight and understanding, and to unhurried reflection upon thoughts, feelings and actions (chapter 9).

7. Individual and collective emotions play an important part in our wider social life, in crowd and group behavior, in consumer activity, in organizational life, in political and artistic preferences, and so on. Reflective personal attitudes brought to bear within those contexts, and in particular situations, contribute to social health (chapter 10).

8. Our passage through life is an unpredictable mix of joys and pains, desires for personal happiness and meaning unbounded. Nobody is perfectly nurtured; all experience 'wounds of the spirit' that call for inner healing. Yet our actions are often misplaced in searching for happiness. Understanding emotions, and matters of human attachment and loss, can be helpful in sustaining us, and those nearby, through phases of low mood, melancholia or depression that interact with fundamental human existential questions (chapter 11).

9. Spiritual development and a holistic life outlook, whether in some specifically religious context or otherwise, interacts with, depends upon, and yet also enables emotional and its associated ethical mastery (chapter 12).

10. A concluding 'epilogue' (chapter 13) addresses matters of living

in grounded hope, and with emotional and ethical poise when, in many practical ways, civilization is fast approaching a global crossroads concerning social and biophysical sustainability. A mass commitment to ecological rationality now seems more than ever necessary, in tandem with new drives towards personal integrity. In the quest for a new, and this time *holistic enlightenment*, grounded in a judicious synthesis of emotion, spirit, body and mind, the bankruptcy of secular materialism is confronted. In that context the reasonable hypothesis of some seriously involved 'First Cause' of creation cannot be avoided. The western archetype, or model, of this divine involvement, that has cradled so much of Western civilization, is Jesus who came as a baby, like one of us. Though the Jesus story is far from being the only example of 'divine involvement' with our human condition, it is a key marker in the evolution of the human idea of Divinity as the embodiment of the compassionate love that history, and much other scholarship, suggests is both our most fundamental need, and indeed purpose. While the nature and practice of love are central in the honing of our emotionality (chapter 7), the thrust of this text is *not* dependent upon acceptance of a divine perspective. However, the healing of hurting emotions in this science-trained author's view is at least partly an issue of 'spiritual grace' available from beyond, yet somehow working within us, if we dare imagine a divine emotional mind (chapter 11).

The remainder of this first chapter briefly sets concern for relational and emotional capability within its contemporary social context.

1.6 An age of relational holocaust

We live in times of awareness of, and for many experience of relational holocaust. If a relational crisis has not overtaken us, then something of the kind is bound to have happened to a friend, neighbor or relative. Until I was well into my twenties, I only knew one divorced and remarried person, an uncle. So far as I can remember, all of my childhood friends in industrial Yorkshire and suburban London in the 1940s and 1950s had two resident parents, apart from those who had lost one in World War Two. Nothing remotely like that type of social stability and security has been possible for the adult generation following mine, let alone that of the contemporary child such as our primary school-aged grandchildren. Many children are anxious about the possibility of their parents' splitting up, and by divorce, even if their family life is seemingly reliable and stable for most of the time.

'Holocaust' in this context is not too strong a word, and I owe it to an experienced child psychiatrist friend. Every time a family, or would-be family disintegrates or experiences severe internal stress, the inner psychic reality is one of social and emotional holocaust. Much of the devastation remains hidden, but is long remembered. Unsurprisingly, workplace and community life and health are affected by relational trauma, however it is caused. A wealth of research now confirms this.

Given the frequent complexity of causation of relational distress and breakdown, there may be no easy or entirely fair 'targets' to blame. Many people are just left with a harsh and even bitter sadness about life, with too often elements of real injustice. Such pains are hard to assuage in a culture of unrealistically high expectations that generally imply that our needs could or should be permanently met by 'a someone'.

If you identify with this last sentence, I hope that you will persevere with this text, even though sometimes that will require courage. We certainly need patience to secure gain from pain, but many find that in holding on through hard times this becomes possible. Meanwhile, be assured that both hope and healing can emerge, sometimes imperceptibly, through deepening our understanding of the many factors that make us who we are.

Relational breakdown frequently happens in a thick fog of hurting and confused emotions, the possibly long antecedents of the collapse unseen, and often sadly unexamined before irrevocable decisions by one or other party are made. Many become discarded or divorced against their considered will, and that can be a brutal form of dis-empowerment. Yet, always, *it takes at least two to make a relationship,* but one to shatter it. It has been both challengingly and well-remarked that:

> There is no democracy in any love relationship, only mercy. Each party, woman, man, the child in each relationship is absolute power as well as absolute vulnerability.'
>
> Adapted from *Love's Work,* Gillian Rose, Chatto and Windus, 1995

Legal processes, perhaps inevitably for most, fail to deliver sufficient principled reparation in too many cases of separation and divorce. Divorce law reform is both a controversial and complex undertaking with many vested interests. Under the burden of caseloads and changing social attitudes, divorce law has shifted much more towards muddling through the consequences rather than examining the causes of breakdown in marital relationships. This of course sets a context for the frequently no less problematic termination of *de-facto* cohabitations. Culpability, a crucial concept in *every* other aspect of law, has more or less disappeared from the divorce lexicon.

One day we may think differently about these matters. But before that can happen a much wider social commitment to relational preparation and sustainability must emerge, even though the evidential need for such investment is already overwhelming. Emotional literacy, and the minding and managing of our emotions are central to all such agenda. Our dominant political and managerial hierarchies rarely consider these issues as crucial elements in mature leadership and policy development.

Meanwhile, society bears a vast burden of mostly private sadness, and sometimes cynicism, concerning wastelands, resulting from relational wars of a very different kind to those in which so many in two World Wars gave their lives in the last century. Collectively, we cannot be proud of some of the ongoing fall out, not least for children. Love and 'charity' really do begin at home, and 'home defense' is every nation's business in winning civic peace and relational prosperity. We have grasped new economic and social freedoms, and in various ways effectively squandered several 'peace dividends', because we have tended to forget that freedom is contingent upon insight and understanding of our 'inward parts'. This truth is captured in the following short poem.

Vigilant Freedom

Freedom is not free,
Not for you, and not for me.
Many gave their lives for freedom's dreams,
So you and I might be freed by their screams.

Freedom without, freedom within,
Means facing our dark side, some call it 'sin'.
Then shining our light side wherever we go,
In parched heat and glistening snow;
Purging catacomb structures, and our dark elves,
Forging integrity in the depths of ourselves;
Keeping a watchfulness, maybe speaking out loud,
Courage to hold fast, even when facing the crowd.

The price of hard-won freedoms, both for you and for me,
Is but one of remembrance, virtue, and vigilance, in all we oversee.
Adapted from *Purpose in Presence*, page 33

Our 'inward parts' are our emotional centers, our 'free-spirit' essences, our hearts and souls. If we are to find better relational ways ahead for ourselves, our children and grandchildren, we need several 'lights' to illuminate these inward parts.

Of course there has never been a golden age of human relating; history and our best literature are witness to that. But our conscious awareness of widespread relational insecurity and pain is relatively new. Many believe strongly that something should be done about this, both structurally in society and in their own lives. This requires nerve, fortitude, patience and persuasiveness, and is ultimately a matter of shifting investment and social values, a truly public matter affecting private realities.

Political anticipation of and responses to this developing social insecurity are and have been meager, lacking strategies that could head off much avoidable pain and dislocation. Much of my professional life has been concerned with such extensive yet avoidable suffering among children, and adults who have responsibility for their emotional and physical safety.

The proper safeguarding of the *social* ecology, which all of us share, is an interlocked story that cannot be explored here. Broad public policy responses are so far inadequate, a part of the problem being that too many leaders, in their unreflective and rushed daily lifestyles, sideline their own emotional material, a reality seen, often vividly, upon their public faces.

Yet now we all need to recognize that there is no way out of the contemporary quagmire of relational unreliability without greatly enhanced individual 'emotional intelligence' and capability concerning our rather capricious and sometimes dangerous feelings. This 'intelligent feeling' is a vital matter for everyone, regardless of social class, narrow IQ, ethnicity, gender, sexual orientation and religious inclination. It also has significance for all in the so-called 'helping professions', including counselors, teachers, medical staffs, politicians and pastors. This is also crucial for those who train such helpers, some at least of whom have not sufficiently resolved elements within their own emotional lives as an ingredient for helping rather than confusing others.

Unresolved emotional pain often perpetuates down the generations, unless the most damaging aspects of habitually impaired relational cycles can be broken through patient new learning. The really good news is that gains in emotional awareness and sensitivity tend to cascade also through relational networks with positive and creative consequences. Negative cycles can be transformed through fresh learning and skills into positive ones that trickle more reliable love within family and community (see further chapters 2 and 8).

1.7 An educational vacuum

Understanding self and other requires emotional literacy. Most formal education concentrates upon developing the mind, the intellectual part of our nature. Significant attention is also given to developing our manipulative 'motor' skills, through such things as science lab-work, physical education and aspects of art, music and technology. The 'intelligence of feeling' has long been sidelined, being absent in most educational standards and paper qualifications debates. Sadly, states of emotions are usually perceived as an accompaniment to the literary aspects of English teaching, or 'soft' material for the difficult or less academically able student, and are marginal instead of central to mainstream learning. Optimizing educational efficiency is a vain enterprise without consideration of the emotional foundations of being.

Governments have been slow to invest seriously in rigorous core courses of Personal and Social Education amid rapid social change, a matter requiring long-term development of well-qualified teachers and political courage to affirm the relevant scholarship. This is a centuries-old, post-reformation and industrial revolution legacy, still largely uninfluenced by our knowledge that *the emotional foundations of all learning and being are crucial for everyone.* School experiences in personal and social education in the UK and elsewhere must be given higher status, and in due course develop much more professional rigor.

The thrust of educational activities is still far too exclusively toward the development of rationality, seen mainly through the head rather than the heart and spirit. Yet all around us we see many different people, including the worldly, intelligent and physically skilled, sometimes behaving very irrationally. For example, whatever our opinions of the President Clinton/Monica Lewinsky 'drama', which so tediously filled our media for months, or of the relational struggles of celebrities, princes, princesses, sports stars and others, here are people, often very capable people, in adolescent emotional fog, distress and need. Their deep emotional longings spill out in confused, risky and 'crazy' behavior, generally to nobody's serious advantage, least of all their own.

Nobody is totally immune from such problems, but fortunately most of us are not exposed to invasive publicity about our every irrational peccadillo of emotional behavior. *Policy must simply recognize that human beings cannot expand arenas of rational behavior without both understanding and actively managing their feelings and emotions.*

Too much of the effort that goes into promoting intellectual reasoning and skills in various forms and fields of knowledge has limited impact, because the emotional dimensions of people's personal and inner lives are neglected and left to chance. Considering the balance of research, there is no way in which educational standards can be sustained, let alone enhanced, without significant changes to the dominant ethos of learning, both through the attitudes and atmospheres of home. This applies particularly to secondary school and college life. The *emotional* climates within which both parents and teachers do their crucial work are the most fundamental factor in these matters. Informed and sensitive public policies must address these issues. Solutions are more to do with opportunities for personal growth and development than extending the tentacles of a 'nanny state' that can seduce citizens into improper forms of dependency.

Unfortunately, too many public, private and charitable administrations have been seduced into a phase of somewhat phony 'objective' accountancy-driven management. In this, emotional factors are usually brushed aside, except for use in marketing and sales. The efficiency costs of such blinkered managerial forms do not feature in accountancy equations, but are huge. Some day we may become wise enough to assess gross local and national *contentment*, rather than 'gross national product' expressed in monetary terms (see also chapter 11). Adam Smith, famed for his economic writings, in his *Theory of Moral Sentiments* (1759), noted that 'the chief part of human happiness arises in the consciousness of being beloved'. Emotional mastery demands that love be factored into all our equations.

1.8 A guiding topic map

While a definitive, universal intellectual map of human feelings and emotions is an unreal notion – because the variety of human experience is simply too vast– it is possible for all of us (yes, all of us) to develop workable models for emotional discourse, personal reflection and more rational overall functioning. Without these we can easily become lost within the apparent morass of our passions, desires, hurts, guilt and prejudices which come and go like irregular and unpredictable tidal waves. This leads to less than optimum life fulfillment, with huge costs to society and ultimately, to world peace.

So what is the scope of the emotional educational territory that we need to come to terms with if we are to become more emotionally literate? Diagram 1 below gives the broad indications, and is reflected in several of the later chapter headings. It is important that readers consider this 'map' now, and refer to it at later points for review.

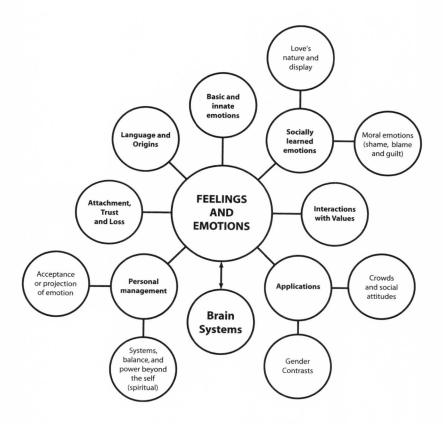

Diagram 1: Feelings and Emotions Topic Map

Our first explicit port of call in relation to this topic map is 'brain systems' from a 'lay' perspective (see chapter 3). Before that we must examine in more detail the scope of human *relational* nature. The whole of the topic map rests within the reality of our social and relational natures, so it is crucial to perceive how this intimately interacts with emotional life.

2
OUR RELATIONAL NATURE: THE EXPRESSIVE FOCUS OF EMOTIONAL LIFE

2

OUR RELATIONAL NATURE: THE EXPRESSIVE FOCUS OF EMOTIONAL LIFE

'It is often sad in relationships, even between people sensitive to each other's moods, that moments of emotion so rarely coincide.'
Adapted from Nan Fairbrother in *An English Year*

'It is on knowledge of the heart, and of the instincts, that reason must establish itself and create the foundation for all its discourse.'
Pascal, 1623-62

Fundamentally, human beings are inter-dependent social 'animals' at the peak of an evolutionary tree that becomes progressively more social in character. It is impossible to imagine becoming or being human without others around to help shape and support us in an interactive mutuality.

Of course there is huge *diversity* in our social relationships in both time investment and opportunity, in 'content' (things shared within the relating), and in the depth and scope of emotion involved. We distinguish, for example, between acquaintances and friends: I smile and share a few words with the several folk (as acquaintances) who deliver our mail, but there is no serious exchange of emotion, though in England we are prone to say how we feel about the weather of the day. With friends, in varying degrees according to closeness, we share more topics, and some of these are likely to be seriously emotional in character. In cohabitation, marriage, parental, and other family relations, the scope is usually wider still if those relationships are properly alive. In sports and leisure activities; in groups or among crowds; as 'consumers'; in interactions with civic authorities or neighbors, or within employment activities, we are able (and most of us do) to experience huge varieties of relating.

More often than not there are important emotions at work in these everyday processes of encounter with others, in which trust is important. These emotional elements, whether or not they are expressed (and a silence may 'speak' emotionally far louder than words!), can often get us into trouble and cause us distress. Such issues may be understood only in relation to our general and specific knowledge of human nature.

2.1 Some human realities: towards knowing ourselves

It is a genuine tragedy that for the most part, educational energy and resources are devoted towards studies of almost everything except the deep nature of the human person, that usually being seen only as narrow psychiatric or counseling areas of specialization. Amid the political drives for short-term measures of educational output there is little early prospect of a profound shift in this skewed orientation. We need to understand that prevailing systems are too subject to the superficial activities of image and presentation.

So let us look at some research-informed *key facts about ourselves*, listed below. In many ways these are backcloths for any serious planning of our lives.

- We are vulnerable, inter-dependent social animals, though many of us have remarkable capabilities of resilience and recovery from hardships.
- Leaving aside the complex matters of genetics, our early experience during fetal development, birthing and infancy is crucial to our ethical, intellectual, emotional and social prospects.

- We are motivated by meaningful survival, rather than survival without some degree of conscious purpose. We are all interested somehow in the purposes and meaning of life, though ultimately we have to find those sufficiently for ourselves.

- In terms of our 'identity' (that is, who we 'say' we are, both to ourselves on the inside track, and for others as descriptions beyond our name), it is clear that we are in a real sense 'nobodies' if we have not got 'committed somebodies'. This simply means that, because we are a social species, we are dependent upon 'significant others' around us in order to become reasonably defined as individuals. As we think of people who are or have been 'committed somebodies' for us, we begin to get close to 'selecting' people who in our feeling and conscious memories have given us, in whatever context, their best attention. These are people through whom we sense we have received reasonably 'reliable love'; of being valued for our own sake. Included here, for those with some sense of religious faith, can be the personhood of 'God', hopefully experienced as a reliable and loving friend.

- Our 'identity' is also defined through cultural traditions of which we are or have been a part, and by both *places* and *objects* that are special to us. For example, though well traveled, my place roots remain in the County of Yorkshire where I was born and lived for all but six of the first twenty-five years of my life. Yet I also have varied attachments to four other family home locations. It is not bizarre to speak of our having 'relationships with objects'. For me these would include my wedding ring, the garden that I have helped to create and maintain over the past fifteen years, books written, and even an old cricket bat and tennis racquet that I have scarcely used in years. I am also very attached to two pairs of brown leather shoes, now many times repaired, and owned for over thirty years; it is important, in more ways than one, for us to be comfortable in our own shoes!

- Given even half a chance, what we most fundamentally believe in, and value, we tend to create around ourselves. What we experience we tend to re-create, often at margins of our awareness, in the next generation. There is now sound evidence of a general human tendency to transmit not only affirmation, but conversely, deprivation. Hence our values in interaction with our experience, are vitally important in shaping our own and others' lives.

- Despite many wonderful insights of science, as a species we retain a marked tendency to irrationality if we assess our own behavior. Too often we are far from safeguarding matters that will secure our own best interests, and those of others, even to the point of survival. For example, in around 90 per cent of transport accidents it is human misjudgments, having a high emotional content, rather than technical failures of the machinery, that trigger disaster. Generally, we are behaving irrationally in relation to both social and biophysical ecosystems, thereby damaging the prospects for future generations, if not our own. Our legacy depends upon what we do with what has been passed onto us. Hence *ecological sustainability, both environmental and social, is for any generation the fundamental collective rational issue.* A sense of reverence for our human nature within Nature is the most rational and responsible foundation value for any society.

This list of seven broad points about our human nature is profound enough for us to pause for the following five-part reflective exercise. Our most unique ability as humans is that of quiet reflection, though too often we allow this to be leeched away by lifestyle pressures, such as 'hurry sickness' and fear of silence, and what might arise from our depths.

Personal exercise 2

- *List the most significant people in your life, and select a few descriptive words to show why each is on your list. Then list some other people whom you imagine might well write down your name in the same circumstances.*
- *What are your first and last memories of being cared for?*
- *Reflect upon both an object and an environmental setting that are of particular importance to you. Try to pin down your reasoning for each selection.*
- *Name two cultural traditions that you believe have contributed to who you are. (For me this includes 'Yorkshire grit', that I translate as a 'dogged persistence').*
- *Note an example of when you have behaved irrationally against your own, and maybe others', best interests. Why do you think you behaved in that manner?*

2.2 Human needs

Beyond having the material necessities of a roof over our heads and sufficient food, drink and sleep, our relational nature gives rise to a few crucial *human needs*. These needs are much more *necessities* for our basic well-being than mere 'wants' or selfish desires. These seemingly universal non-material necessities for both adults and children may be expressed as four areas as follows:

In order to thrive, beyond surviving, humans need:

1. Reliable love

Reliable love and attention from at least one other person. Such love and attention is the basis for social and civic affirmation, and includes being comforted when distressed (see chapter 7).

Reliable love is the most fundamental requirement for our safe emotional development. As the regular, committed and unselfish attention of another is experienced, the foundations of trust form, and also the reasonable prospect of later becoming a considerate person oneself.

It is difficult for us to place ourselves in another's shoes if we have not experienced *and felt* ourselves to be the subject of that sort of consideration. Research (let alone common sense) shows that the sooner this happens in our lives the better.

Beyond the toddler stage, the 'civic' component begins to register as a growing range of social memberships beyond close family care become experienced, for example through a judicious but not pervasive range of organized pre-school activities.

It is important to note here that without the development of *social trust* and reciprocity, family, community and democratic life become impossible. Growing such social trust begins in the womb and soon thereafter, and remains by far our world's biggest challenge. Secure loving slowly brings individual beauty of character into being.

2. New, understandable experience

New experiences that are intelligible, or become so through explanation and teaching.

This need reflects our nature and status as lifelong learners, and, in consequence, our need for guiding teachers, drawn from a far wider range of people than those paid by society in that role. Here we should note that new, stimulating experience is of no help to us if it is not understandable in relation to our stage of development. Indeed stimulating material may be positively harmful and/or frightening, especially if there are no others around to explain what is going on, and whether it is fact or fiction. Young children watching TV or videos without supervision is, for example, a very risky venture.

3. *Praise and encouragement*
Praise and encouragement in worthy and worthwhile endeavors.
Everyone needs appropriate challenge, and encouragement and praise for their best efforts in any worthy situation. A regular atmosphere of criticism or cynicism de-motivates and demeans people, feeding negative aspects of our emotions, and undermining inner confidence. Teachers who regularly show warmth, and give regular but discriminating praise to their students, tend to be popularly respected and achieve better learning outcomes than those who are too often cold and critical. Implicit here is praise for the praiseworthy, and raises questions not only about what is a 'good effort' in human terms, but whether it is an effort in the direction of a general good, and is therefore a matter of worthwhile values and virtues (see section 2.5 following).

4. *A measure of individual responsibility.*
Personal and social responsibility, appropriate to individual circumstances and capability.
We learn to be responsible by being given attention from good role models, and by being given appropriate responsibility, initially of course under watchful but not over-intrusive guidance. If we have faith in someone's ability to respond, they are more likely to behave with responsibility. To be denied a level of responsibility matched to our experience is not only very frustrating, but likely to lead to resentments with anti-social consequences. Older mentors in authority, including sensitive parents, understand that this requires some well judged risk-taking to secure others' growth within this arena of basic need.

Table 1 expands these four areas of needs, illustrated at three broad phases of the life: infancy, youth/adolescence and adulthood. The continuity of many of these needs is noteworthy, and more is given concerning life phases in section 3.1.

Table 1: Core life-course human needs in outline

Babyhood/Infancy	Youth/Adolescence	Adulthood*
To be welcomed as unique and loved in a secure home base	Patient consideration and understanding within this child to adult transition	On-going appreciation, sharing, caring encouragement and support
Cuddles and strokes	Bodily affirmation amid a transitional identity	Hugs and touching affirmations
Eye contact conveying a hopeful reciprocity	Reciprocity with some economic discretion	Friendship amid sufficient economic security
Close, warm and eye-focused feeding	Regular family meals and some flexibility in routine	Relaxed eating and conversation
Warmth, play and praise	Firmness and tolerance	Warmth and praise
To stretch and kick	Safe energy release	Sufficient exercise
Sleep for growth	Sleep, and awakenings	Sufficient sleep
Attentive comfort in distress and mess	Patient comfort for probed distress	Comfort in distress and disappointment
Stimulation from safe, colorful objects	Someone to listen rather than to program	Stimulation through new perspectives and interests
Tender speaking, singing and comforting music	Some controlled personal space for expression	Personal space for reflection and relaxation

*Adult phases include the roles of parent, carer and citizen

2.3 Relational and emotional intelligence

Relatively recently, psychologists have conceded that intelligence, perceived traditionally as solely a matter of intellectual capability, should be reconfigured as something of much greater variety than has been crudely assessed by IQ tests since the 1930s. Such commonsense has been long overdue, and is now seen to have some scientific basis. It has, for example, been suggested that IQ (intellectual intelligence, or, rather, mental agility) contributes no more than about 20 per cent to those many factors that determine what may be seen as overall success in life. For example, it is of limited value to have a very high IQ, or even be an internationally revered scholar or musician, if one cannot sustain a relationship, take 'time out' for recreation, or if one is regularly depressed.

We have needed a wider theory of human talents for a long time. Consequently a number of other dimensions to intelligence are now in the process of being legitimized. Here we need to be concerned with two of these: *relational* and *emotional* intelligence. These may be simply defined as the following potential human abilities or capabilities:

RI – *self and other relational intelligence* includes the abilities to:

- form an accurate model of oneself, and to use it effectively in life; and

- understand other people, their motivations and working processes so as to be able to work cooperatively with them.

EI – *self and other emotional intelligence* includes:

- having knowledge of and being able to access one's own feelings, to discriminate amongst them, and able to draw upon and manage feelings to guide optimum behavior, and

- recognizing, discerning and responding appropriately to the moods, temperaments, emotions, motivations and desires of other people.

This book aims to progress readers' emotional intelligence (EI) along the two avenues stated. One consequence is that the two relational intelligence (RI) elements will almost certainly be simultaneously enhanced. In both RI and EI it should be noted that there are *self* and *other* components. This is an indissoluble interconnection, reflecting our social inter-dependence.

Table 2 summarizes our overall human *relational dimension* as five segments involving people, places and objects. Implied here is that balanced relational literacy and living involves commitment and attention to each of these five aspects of our being.

Table 2: Five Dimensions of the Human Relational Self

	Form of relationship	*Focus of relationship includes*
1	Self with self	Self-knowledge, self-worth + self-respect
2	Self with significant others (May include the Divine dimension)	The caring of others + the cared-for self (Also, appropriately expressed, the sexual self)
3	Self with significant objects	Attachment/identity tokens
4	Self with environment	Roots and spatial respect
5	Self with society	Citizenship and vocational self*

*Implies useful work and mutual service opportunities for all in society

Even though there are varying degrees of emotionality within each of these segments of relatedness, the emotional dimension is pervasive, so that relational literacy and living is hugely dependent upon emotional mastery.

By way of review, we may reconfigure the elements of EI and RI, as outlined above, as *'self'* with *'other'* intelligence (SI and OI if you wish), described as follows:

Self intelligence comprises essentially three elements:

- Gaining an accurate self-knowledge, plus a capacity to form a model of that self and then to use it in active living.

- Having access to and awareness of one's own feelings and an ability to discriminate amongst them.

- Being able to draw upon one's own identified feelings so as to guide personal behavior.

Interpersonal intelligence embodies:

- An ability to understand other people, what motivates them, how they function, and how to work cooperatively with them.

- The capacity both to discern and to respond appropriately to the emotions, moods, temperament, and legitimate desires of others.

Note that each of these features calls for significant space for calm reflection upon experience.

2.4 Developmental experience of attachment

It is most important for us to recognize where our relational nature and emotional life begins: way back in the womb. We all literally began when the sperm-fertilized ovum from our biological parents' became securely bound, 'bonded' and 'attached' to our mother's uterine wall. From the start we are therefore a species 'attached', and the concept of *attachment* provides helpful insights in studies of human development and relationships.

From conception, the *attachment* process ensures our physical survival. Both fetus and infant are essentially helpless, and must command sufficient warmth, protection and nurture for survival. Until the moment of birth, the womb provides these three essential forms of care, especially if mother has good health habits and a generally positive psychological attitude towards the pregnancy.

Then, beyond baby's first breath, and the severing of the umbilical cord, new 'hands-on' means of giving warmth, nurture and protection must arise through forms of bodily contact that are emotionally encouraging and convey real feelings of an inclusive security. Baby simply needs to feel welcomed, safe and wanted in this strange new world. Every baby is programmed to long for total acceptance of its state of being, within a secure environmental home base. Babies tend to respond positively to what they sense as an all-loving, all-knowing, all-protective and powerful being, such as a loving and well-supported mother.

If the child's emotional needs are neglected, psychological growth shaped within brain circuitry (see chapter 3) may be stunted to the point that, if it were physically evident, it would be alarming. So young children need to be carefully observed in terms of the viability of their attachment behavior to their prime carers, most usually mother, emotionally and practically supported by father and a small number of others, as well as through regular checks of their physical development.

An infant's emotional needs regularly met by a natural, reciprocal (two-way) bond, first with mother, tend to result in a fairly smooth passage through both physical and psychological developmental stages (see following section 3.1). The child thereby acquires essential experiences of secure attachment and trust that assist in establishing sound relationships in the future. Because baby both *feels* and then knows (in that order) its value to mother, then a few others, self-esteem grows as the foundation of happiness and, later, moral strength and inner contentment. Being able to rely on affection and care, baby (then, later, child, youth and adult) experiences and feels consideration from close others. This endows basic trust that builds confidence in and, later, respect for others.

The flip side of attachment is separation, and sometimes loss and bereavement. These contrasting features intermingle over all phases of the life cycle. Interestingly one index of the quality of infant attachment lies in evaluating what happens when the prime parental attachment figure leaves and, later, returns to the child. Sound attachment achieves safe separation, without panic or clinging. Healthy attachment is not akin to a rigid bond of parental superglue, for that would be to deny the physical and wider individuality of both parties. Good parenting encourages safe, staged separation over time, a delicate process both during infancy, and much later at the important yet under-estimated developmental and now often extended phase of leaving home. The need for a secure base, offering comfort in distress, is balanced by the need to have fresh stimulation through fresh personal exploration that wise parents do not over-control, but nonetheless endeavor to make reasonably safe. Human exploration always has risks that need judging by those exercising care according to context, age and capacity.

The often hidden distress of poor early bonding, and enforced or premature separation can be intense. If secure attachment is not modeled, established and enjoyed, there is a felt sense of insecurity about that crucial commodity, love (see chapter 7). Then pathological jealousies, anger, attention-seeking and power hunger are likely to arise, and can have disastrous effects upon later relationships and civic life. If anger is turned inwards, the resulting depression (a state of mind-mood often linked with unexpressed anger) may later lead to social withdrawal, substance abuse or promiscuous, loveless sex in a vain attempt to find relief and succor. For example, some young women seek pregnancy in a desperate attempt to have a child of their own, who might love them without condition. However, babies only learn about love through the ways in which their carers behave.

Healthy attachment makes it possible to achieve a gradual and mature separation from parental figures. The cutting of the umbilical cord immediately after birth is involuntary as far as the baby is concerned. At that time, however, the physical link of the cord is not necessary for oxygen supply to the baby's blood, because independent breathing has started. The first *voluntary separation* occurs when a baby crawls away from mother, confident of a return to her safely when ready. Later leavings and returns, as baby gets older, grow from this, and cannot be programmed in advance by mothers or at their convenience. If separations for which the child is not emotionally ready are insisted upon, such as premature weaning from the breast or the too early use of alternative childcare due to employment demands, baby will tend to interpret and internalize them as rejection or indifference. Such negative feelings can set deeply imprinted, and generally unconscious, patterns for the rest of a person's life.

Independence, or less dependence, if that is what parents want the growing child to achieve, *cannot be forced,* and there can be major differences in readiness for this development even in the same family. We can only become independent by outgrowing each stage appropriately. Thus our separations may be viewed as necessary rites of passage in growing up, eventually to leave home without too much distress, and, importantly, having the desire to revisit home of origin in comfort rather than under duress. This is a widely underestimated transition in late adolescence or young adulthood.

Healthy and secure growth through each stage of life usually prepares us for adjustment to the next. Ironically, parental attachment that is reluctant to allow a timely separation for their offspring (e.g. on starting school, some freedom at adolescence or leaving home) may indicate unmet needs and fears of parents. Good bonding is not to be associated with rigidity or an over-protective style that can overwhelm children. Within bounds, flexibility of parental response is an aspect of secure attachment.

Throughout life most of us experience a natural ambivalence about attachment and separation. Sometimes we want to be close and friendly; at others we wish to feel free and have space of our own, not least with people we love. This is a healthy part of our individuality. However, we should always aim to take respectful care over our attachments and separations, since they tend to echo within emotional experience through whole lifetimes, a reality that is encountered further in this text.

The innocence and simplicity of being accepted in our human nakedness, of body, mind, emotions and soul, in sharing and mutual recognition, is what human beings long for right from birth as the antidote to the possibility of loneliness, desolation, and personal insolvency. Yet so often we fight shy of discussing this fundamental necessity, even though it has massive implications for ordering the paths of our relatively short lives, in which our own choices combine with subtle coercions of market forces and social habits.

Social and educational policies need to plan for and to respect secure attachments. The goal should be to deliver for everyone, as early in life as possible, copious experiences of genuine, regular, predictable, human contact. Such a basic human right comes through 'minds-on and hands-on' staple and stable diets for emotional health in the early years, which also emerge as a therapeutic key for calming and resolving subsequent emotional difficulties.

Table 3 gives, in summary, some contrasting feelings concerning human attachment.

Table 3: Common feelings associated with contrasts in attachment

Secure and healthy attachment	Insecure attachment, felt as loss
comfortable and close	discomfort and aloneness
warm and glowing	chilled numbness
calm and beneficial	stress and distress
feeding and nourishing	emptiness and hunger
attractive and healing	hurt and anger
enlarged and accepted	diminished and lost
secure and safe	insecure and unsafe

Personal Exercise 3

Looking back on your life, who was the most important mother figure and father figure for you? Record brief notes about this, and your associated feelings. (Someone other than either of your parents can of course be named.)

2.5 Values and virtues

It has been mentioned that issues of *values as well as emotions* permeate many elements of our relational capability. These two areas actually interact, because we find that many of the things we find ourselves feeling strongly about are related to *values* that we have acquired through a combination of upbringing, discussion and later, personal choice. Though our values and make up certainly affect our emotions, on occasion we might decide to shift our values somewhat in order to accommodate new insights into the emotional dimension. Where there is little overlap in value systems, there is no secure basis for relationship, let alone intimacy. Equally, developing a human relationship involves an exploration of values; those issues which underpin and then extend a person's essential being, motivations and inner commitments.

Our personal values are essentially what matters most to us, what we regard as ultimately valuable, and which we will spend time and effort both to achieve and to defend. Their potential range is in practice vast, and values can vary in level of detail. For example, valuing high employment rates, or warm and stable family relationships would prompt, on the one hand, inward investment and job creation schemes, and on the other creating conditions whereby parents can spend quality focus and relaxation time with their children.

Our personal values, involving their emotional content, arise from many influences. These include family and educational experience, religion, mass media, peer pressures, civic law and tradition. The mass media now play a significant part in the way we both value and experience the world, and we certainly need sharp critical faculties to evaluate the reliability, depth, poise and wisdom of their outpourings.

Despite much fragmentation in contemporary culture, fortunately there still seems to be considerable consensus about core values, reflecting perhaps our deeply ingrained sense that we should aim to behave as we would like others to treat us. This is the so-called golden rule of '*Do as you would be done by*'. In a 2005 UK Channel 4 survey of some 40,000 respondents for a two-hour-long television program on contemporary ethical 'commandments', that particular value gained a staggering four times the votes of any amongst the sample top twenty. It is unsurprising therefore that the following values are broadly respected, and are variously tapped in devising group and institutional mission statements, and at least some organizational practices and reward systems:

Honesty and fair play	Calm respect for others	Non-violence
Keeping promises	Making apology	Forgiveness
Physical self-care	Reasonable self-denial	Punctuality

Demonstrations of such values in organizations that seriously implement them will tend to bring praise and encouragement; one of our basic needs (section 2.2). If such values are not displayed in actual behavior, offence may be caused within the group and community setting, resulting in negative consequences of emotion, including cynicism and, sometimes, disciplinary action.

Interestingly, in the TV-related survey referred to, 'taking responsibility for your own actions' was rated second to top, that is, the number two, modern 'commandment'. This suggests that despite tendencies within some bureaucratic procedures to mask personal accountabilities, many do not wish to live in 'a blame someone else', shameless and guilt-free type of society.

There is however, no simple relation between values and behavior. Our highest aspirations sometimes elude us. Sincerely held values, and the practice of noble virtues such as honesty, prudence, compassion and moderation, properly constrain and often make demands upon our actions. However, it is not necessarily easy to live up to our values, and when we so fail we tend to feel shame and guilt (which are 'moral emotions', see chapters 6 and 11). If we aspire to be perfectionists, with all the anxieties that tend to go along with that trait, such guilt may become oppressive.

Naturally, our social and even professional reputation may be threatened, and others' respect for us may decline when we are clearly seen to fail to live up to our expressed values. Also, for most people, inner self-respect, including a calm conscience, is dependent upon a reasonably good match between personal values and behavior. However, hidden emotional issues, yet to be resolved within a person's biography, may undermine an ideal consistency.

While it is reasonable that others' trust in us requires a fairly good fit between what we say, as a reflection of our values, and what we do, it is probably unreasonable to expect a perfect fit between values and behavior. No statement of value will give us a simple formula for how we should act in every life situation. There are in practice many situations of moral dilemma in life. These often require a weighing of evidence, and some emotional, spiritual and intellectual battle before a sufficient resolution can be found. Such dilemmas can be an ultimate test of character and integrity, drawing upon the well of human virtues, such as discernment, courage and compassion. Such virtues may be seen as those characteristics or character traits that enable us to live up to our values.

Yet all these issues are related in complex ways to the functioning of our central nervous system, and to the development of our heart-linked brains. It is to this that we now turn after a fourth (optional) exercise. Here it is proper to note that human beings cannot realistically be viewed as simply biological machines. Biology has not begun to explain *the evolution of emotional connectedness*. Our emotional sensitivity and automatic mutual empathy, along with our feel for ethics and spirituality, suggest that we are base-programmed to be highly cooperative and trusting, despite the fact that modern life so often appears to deny and to dent both this hope and yearning.

Personal Exercise 4

1. *Devise a short list of what you think has become your own core values. Who seems to have most influenced these, and which of these values has been the most difficult for you to uphold?*

2. *Record three examples of other peoples' behavior that upsets you or makes you angry. What, fundamentally, causes that reaction in you?*

3. *In your own present behavior patterns what causes you most distress, and why? How do you work on this, if at all?*

3
EMOTIONS WITHIN BRAIN DEVELOPMENT AND FUNCTION

3
EMOTIONS WITHIN BRAIN DEVELOPMENT AND FUNCTION

*'The brain is the interpreter of consciousness as well
as the mediator of feelings.'*
Hippocrates, 400 BC

'Emotion has taught mankind to reason.'
Marquis de Vauvenargues, 1715-47

*'Feeling, which comes more easily to children than adults,
is surely something a computer could never have.'*
Sir Roger Penrose

This chapter mainly offers a basic introduction concerning the human brain's function in relation to our emotional life, with a minimum of technical terms. Some of the findings of modern neuro science can help us to understand ourselves, and our varied ways of behaving towards each other.

The human brain is each person's central control system over three broad areas of life:

- the coordination, through the central nervous system, of our body-brain functioning, including heartbeat, of our manipulative or motor skills and sexual expression;

- thinking or 'cognition', imaging and imagining (meaning mental representations of the real and 'possible' environment, and events); and

- social relations, emotions, personality and moral sensibility.

However, the brain's development is set within the broader context of phases of human development over the life cycle that are first summarized. This summary (section 3.1) links with the relational and 'needs' issues covered in chapter 2.

3.1 Types and phases of human development

Human growth, development and maturing may be divided broadly into *two interacting strands: types* and *phases* of development. The types are distinctive aspects of our basic human nature and are neatly summarized as follows:

The six distinctive, and interacting types of human development

Physical, sensory and motor	Social and personality	Emotional (innate and learned)
Intellectual (several forms)	Moral and ethical	Spiritual and faith

Our physical development, including brain development (following sections), includes the five basic senses of sight, hearing, touch, taste and smell, and the ability to move body parts both consciously (as in holding a cup, or kicking a ball), or unconsciously (as in breathing or blinking). Intellectual (thinking) development involves a handful of distinctive basic forms: mathematical, linguistic, scientific and aesthetic for example. Emotional development can be understood within a framework of innate and learned emotions (see later, chapter 5).

Studies in differing cultural environments have shown that the human life-course has a number of common stages. This is unsurprising, for we are after all members of the same species, sharing the same basic chromosome structure upon which a myriad of genetic variations become superimposed.

The main cumulative *phases of human development*, and their associated prime developmental tasks, are shown table 4 below. Perusal of this table may identify the stage or stages that best describe your present sense of life. Most of the dimensions of our individual human development are not precisely related to chronological age. There may be periods of reversion to earlier phases, such as a mid-life crisis that is often adolescent in nature. Hence the age ranges shown are only guidelines.

Individual life prospects tend to be related to the basic level of success in meeting each stage's core developmental tasks shown in the table. Development does not happen in a personal vacuum. At all stages, apart from maybe the last, development is no less a social than an individual achievement. Each of the staged developmental tasks includes intellectual, emotional, social, moral and spiritual types listed previously. Where the fulfillment of developmental tasks lags significantly, some catching up at later chronological phases becomes necessary if an adequate life is to be sustained. So, for example, many of the mid-life crisis transitions experienced by significant proportions of men and women are in many respects predictable. Yet we have rarely been taught to reflect in advance on such matters, that if not handled carefully, tend to have major outfall costs.

Stage	Age guide	Core Developmental Tasks
Embryo	Up to 9 months	Safe growth towards, and through, the birth event.
Babe-infant	0–18 months	Learning to relate and to trust, mainly through touch, feeding as a social experience, sight, and sounds. Learning to trust.
Toddler	1.5–3 years	Exploring the physical and social world.
Child	4–11 years	Developing mental, physical and social skills.
Adolescent	12–18 years	Exploring and establishing a separate social, personal and sexual identity, both in and beyond home.
Young adult	19–25 years	Creating personal and civic roles, particularly from employment options, community activities, and the possibilities of cohabitation and mating.
Nested adult	26–35 years	Establishing the personal world of own home, partnering, parenting and employment career.
Mid-life	36–49 years	Latent chance to re-establish personal identity; may involve a partial retreat to adolescence.
Cruise-time	50-59 years	Experience of relaxed being, in established roles.
Retirement	60 to 75	Relishing life with opportunities for new fulfillment.
Old age	Over 75 years	Becoming pensive as a reflector of wisdom and light; a sense of completion and acceptance of death emerges.

Table 4: Basic Human Life-Cycle Stages

Personal Exercise 5

Looking at each of the six distinctive, and interacting types of human ddevelopment listed on page 49, give yourself, as you believe you are now, a rating of high, medium or low, and commenting on each. Here is a sample tabular record.

Human Development Type	Rating	Comment
Physical, sensory and motor	High	Good at ball sports and do-it-yourself tasks.
Social and personality	Medium	Quite balanced, but occasionally withdrawn.
Emotional (innate and learned)	Low	Moods variable; have a temper but do not talk about it.
Intellectual (several forms)	High	Passed key exams; good at math; quick on new uptake.
Moral and ethical	Medium	Always struggle with expenses claims and income tax.
Spiritual and faith	Low	Tend to be cynical here. Do not pray or go to churches.

3.2 The character of the human brain

The human brain, present as a living set of organs throughout the life phases outlined, and capable of the six basic types of development, seems beyond doubt the most complex and remarkable coordinating device on earth. At birth our brains have about 100 billion nerve cells (neurons) and a trillion honeycombed glial cells, gluing, protecting and nourishing them. A single neuron may receive signals from as many as 10,000 other neurons, so that the potential number of electro-chemical connections between the neurons in a single brain is greater than all the particles in the universe. This is an awesome reality, not simply for modern neuroscientists but for us all, as we go about the experience of ordinary living, carrying with us extraordinary 'equipment', head-high!

The brain is the supervising control centre of the central nervous systems for all vertebrates. It controls conscious behaviors such as walking, opening a door and thinking, and most involuntary, or unconscious behavior including breathing and reactions to intrusive pain. The brain functions by receiving information from nerve cells from every part of the body, assessing the data, and then sending directives to the muscles and glands, or simply storing the information in vast memory banks. The information is in the form of electrical and chemical signals that move through brain circuits networked through the billions of neurons.

The scale of the brain's internal structural elements, and its outreach to and from the whole central nervous system, can be grasped in some part from the following *descending order of size*; this is given as factor multiples of ten by which one meter (39.3 inches) – which is the order of scale of the whole central nervous system, tip to toe – must be divided:

Central nervous system	Scale of about one meter (39.3 inches)	Division: factors of ten
Neural systems	1m divided by: 10	1
Neural maps	100	2
Neural networks	1,000	3
Neurons (brain nerve cells)	10,000	3
Synapses (brain cell connections)	1,000,000	6
Large molecules	1,000,000,000	9
Atoms and small molecules	10,000,000,000	10

Descending order of size of brain's structural elements

In seeking to describe the human brain, many have made the analogy with the computer. However, the human brain is not like a computer waiting to be switched on and keyed so as to perform its tricks, for it starts to function long before being 'finished'. But neither is it ever 'finished' in an absolute sense, as is a computer whose basic motherboard can take no more upgrade parts, for the brain is a *living* complex of organs. The brain's hugely complex and dynamic 'wiring' pattern does not stabilize from the outline fetal and birth blueprint for several years.

Each human brain has, like the rest of the body, its given genetic coding (*nature*) from our biological parents. However, its detailed form and capability is hugely affected by the quality of its environmental experience (*nurture*), as it grows in the womb, and both during and beyond birth. Tender loving care and huge varieties of stimulation affect the ways in which neurons connect to create operational brain circuitry. *Nurture* works through *nature* to build long-term memory, with repeated experience providing wiring (or re-wiring), knitting neurons into circuits, with great plasticity and readiness to learn, and thereby to change. The potential number of neural connections is greater than all the particles in the universe! Experience then becomes the chief architect of the 'useful brain' as a mind, within windows of developmental opportunity for movement, sight, hearing, emotions, and language. However, basic 'hard-wired' changes beyond puberty, though possible, are (as many of our remedial professions know), difficult to achieve.

Hence it is no longer appropriate, if it ever was, to view the newborn brain as a blank slate at the mercy of a competing environment. Rather it is a biological organism in an interactive *dance* with its total environment begun around three weeks into fetal gestation. This involves a metamorphosis at least as complex as that of larva to butterfly with, at the molecular level, long migration of neurons within the brain during fetal growth.

The brain is first an emotional system, before it emerges also as a thinking and moral system as a result of varied social interactions. It is awesome to imagine that something so simple as regular, and secure cuddles, and the presence of someone we trust to soothe our distress when we are very young, actually changes the developing brain's circuits and electrochemistry. The sad corollary to that is that the absence of regular and sensitive nurture will send brain development on some different tacks, and certain circuits helpful to the social organism will not form or will atrophy. It seems that a general principle applies to brain circuits, much the same as that for our muscle capability, namely, if not fed, exercised and practiced, there is decay; in other words, 'use it or lose it'!

Now, as we move on to matters of brain structure and circuitry we note by way of review that the brain's control functions:

- relay and record masses of data for and from our senses
- govern the manipulation of our bodies (motor co-ordination)
- make possible our thoughts (cognition), our imaginations and dreams
- oversee our social relationships, reflecting and expressing personality within them
- house our conscience, and our integrity (moral capacity), and
- drive our emotional lives.

Socially and educationally we need to remember that, for the most part, *our brains and being are born curious,* and with vast potential capabilities. The practical challenges of nurture, socialization and education are to *ensure that we stay curious,* and so develop creatively.

3.3 Outline of brain circuit development

This is not a medical textbook. However, four simplified diagrams, and a handful of technical terms (mainly of anatomical parts and which need not be committed to memory) help us to understand the basic character of the brain's systems that drives everything important about us, including our emotions. Such basic understanding, that also opens our awe, reinforces the necessity of our 'taking care' of ourselves, and each other, as delicate, capable and wondrous social beings having so much more potential than we dare to imagine.

Before we look at the basic anatomical layout of the brain and its components in section 3.4 below, this section outlines a few further aspects of brain circuitry. At a microscopic level this is very relevant to our emotional life, and to the thinking and behavior that it empowers, or de-rails, and with which it interacts.

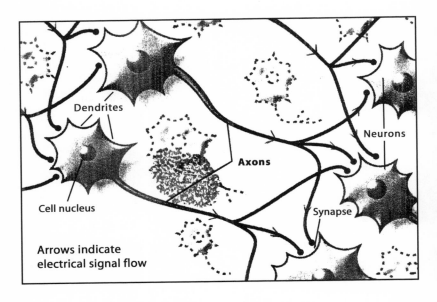

Diagram 2: Wiring of the brain in progress

Diagram 2 shows in two dimensions (not the reality of three), some initial connections forming between neurons in the embryo. Neurons have different shapes, such as the star-shaped ones in the diagram that reach out in all directions; others are long and thin, and send snaking 'feelers' to far reaches of the body, while others have a dense branching crown and antler-like protrusions. The long-distance transmission lines of the human nervous system, called 'axons', spin out multiple branches from the neuron centers or 'cell nuclei'. These then connect with many targets called 'dendrites' on the surfaces of other neurons. These connections enable the transmission of electrical signals through the axons to the dendrite receiver sites.

Zooming in, almost further than the scale of diagram 2 (but also shown), reveals a tiny gap of about one millionth of a meter (a micron) where each axon meets a dendrite; this is called a synapse. Minute electrical currents cross the synapses when the axons secrete chemicals known as neurotransmitters that are triggered when the neuron cells are appropriately 'fired-up'. Then a kind of chain reaction develops between millions of connected cells, and we move to the threshold of a 'mind event', this being a complex combination of past brain memory and the present totality of our environment. These 'events' then form the basis of all our thinking skills (such as doing numerical addition), our learned behavior such as walking and talking, and our moods, feelings and emotions.

After birth, brain size grows rapidly, for it can do so safely now that baby's curved-plate-like skull will not again have to become flexed, even 'squashed' during passage down and along the mother's birth canal. The new flood of sensory experiences from a strange outside world triggers intense electrical activity. This extends and fine-tunes the brain's circuitry during the early days, months and years of life.

A measure of this explosion of brain function and capability can be imagined from the more than tripling of brain mass in the year from birth. The average baby's brain weight at birth is 350 grams, while at age 12 months it is 1,100 grams. It has been estimated that about 60 per cent of a baby's energy intake from its feeding during the first year of life is used to construct neural networks. During this time, brain development takes huge precedence over physical mobility. So from the brain comes all the gain!

The long delay in the independent mobility of humans after birth compared with the rest of the animal kingdom is no accident, for it is during this time, in both waking and sleeping, that building brain capability is the priority. Indeed, it has been found that even in severely undernourished children and adults that other organs tend to be harmed well before the brain. The brain seems to have 'bounce-back' capability, though not indefinitely. Severely deprived children's neural development seems not to be able to fully 'catch-up' in normal growth beyond about 6 to 12 months of impoverished material and emotional conditions. All stages of human development are important, but the first year or two of life is a crucial window, forming the character of many mental templates for later life.

As already noted, a key principle of the many elements of brain function at any stage seems to be 'use it or lose it'. Hence the importance of appropriate stimulation and 'exercise' as a core human need, as discussed in the previous chapter, section 2.2. This extends to all parts of the central nervous system, such as the functioning of our eyes, including peripheral vision. More stimulation increases the electro-chemical connections (brain 'synapses') between the 100 billion neurons. This process is an amazing metamorphosis involving the long migration of neurons during fetal growth. Some neurons become lodged to thrive in the heart, an organ that operates as more than a mere blood pump, much ancient literature having spoken of the heart as the seat of human emotions, and still widely symbolized in, for example, Valentine Day rituals.

During childhood, much extension and filling-in of neural circuits takes place as the emotional 'heart-mind-in-the-making' emerges. However, after about the age of ten, ruthless pruning of unutilized neural connections (synapses) takes place, leading to less plasticity, though strangely increasing the brain's focused capability. This focusing works for both good and ill, depending upon the emergent hard-wired through-nurture processes, or ones of sensed emotional neglect. So more rigid 'mind sets' are by this stage becoming established.

This reality gives insight concerning why it becomes much

more difficult to rescue severely anti-social children beyond the primary school phase, why most youth delinquency can be predicted by the age of about eight years old, and why habitual criminal behavior is unlikely to change without in-depth educational and therapeutic interventions. Though there are many individual variations, trends of mental and social health or sickness have been set in place before the start of secondary education. Tackling social stresses surrounding parenthood that affect the development of neural systems in childhood for regulating emotional learning, motivation and memory is therefore vital, yet much neglected in public welfare.

The brain is kept functioning through the beating of the heart that pumps 25 billion red blood cells, oxygenated from the air via the lungs' breathing, around the human body every 20 seconds. Over an average lifetime the human heart beats 2.5 billion times, triggered by electrical signals from the brain, and sometimes influenced by stresses of many kinds. So our heart-brain system is an awesome interactive combination!

3.4 The basic physical layout of the brain

In discussing brain circuitry, there are important anatomical aspects to be considered. The brain is a multi-component organ, almost, but not quite 'twin-engined' insofar as almost all the components are doubled-up as left and right sides. The whole brain is about as big as a coconut or cantaloupe melon, with the twin-halved shape of a walnut, the consistency of chilled butter, and the color of uncooked liver. The brain's various parts receive a mostly common form of blood supply.

For centuries it has been known that the main and most massive part of the human brain, the cortex, rests under the top of the protective skull and above a much smaller mass of complex tissue, the limbic system, close to the top of the spinal chord (see diagram 3 below). The whole brain floats in protective fluid, and the cortex has two front-to-back, left and right lobes, both wrinkled on the surface.

These lobes, with their various fore and aft sections, are interconnected by complex tissue called the *corpus callosum*. This has some 145 millions of nerve fibers whose function is to keep the left and right lobes in communication. People can survive with this connective left-right tissue severed and lead lives of reasonable quality. Such surgical operations have been used to control severe epilepsy, indicating that in respects we have two brains that can function to some degree apart.

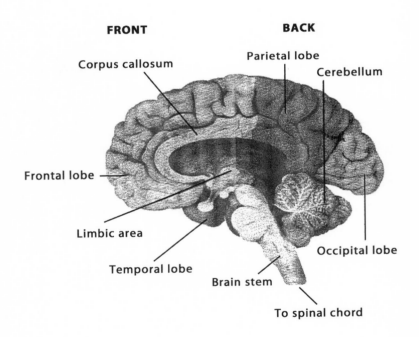

Diagram 3: Section through the brain
(from front to back of cortex)

Much more recently, neuroscientists have been greatly aided by modern imaging techniques that sensitively scan the brain without harm. In consequence, it is possible to be reasonably specific about which parts of the cortical lobes operate in different practical functions such as hearing, vision, movement, language and so on. Most of those site designations, informed from brain scans conducted under a wide variety of conditions, need not concern us here. We need to bear in mind however that the mapping of the 'over' (cortical) and 'under' (limbic) brain is in detail still relatively provisional, somewhat akin to cartographers' views of our world around the sixteenth century.

The two lobed cortical halves of the human brain seem to have different balances of strength and weakness, with distinctive means of processing, suggesting that there are some 'hard-wiring' features. The left side is strong upon analytic thinking, calculation, language and intellectual precision. The right side tends to be more dreamy and holistic, having rather more strength in non-verbal patterns of spatial form, melody, feelings and emotions. These distinctions may sometimes be oversimplified, with the left cortical brain described as more masculine, and the right as more feminine. While there are gender differences in brain structure (see chapter 9), the two main cortical lobes interact and overlap in functions far more than this implies.

One feature is that there are a number of lateral crossovers in brain functioning, For example, for vision, which is processed by two occipital lobes at the rear of the twinned cortex (see diagram 3), the right eye's signals are processed by the left hemisphere and vice-versa. Only for our sense of smell through the olfactory bulbs (see diagram 4) is this lateral crossover not seen. Handedness, by way of further example, seems to be established quite early in fetal gestation and is mostly set up by birth. About 10 per cent of people experience varieties of left-handedness, indicative of some right brain dominance, and tend to show more variety in brain organization than right-handed, left hemisphere-dominant people.

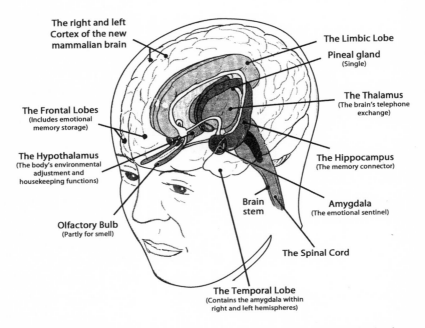

The right and left Cortex of the new mammalian brain

The Limbic Lobe

Pineal gland
(Single)

The Thalamus
(The brain's telephone exchange)

The Frontal Lobes
(Includes emotional memory storage)

The Hypothalamus
(The body's environmental adjustment and housekeeping functions)

The Hippocampus
(The memory connector)

Brain stem

Amygdala
(The emotional sentinel)

Olfactory Bulb
(Partly for smell)

The Spinal Cord

The Temporal Lobe
(Contains the amygdala within right and left hemispheres)

Diagram 4: Representation of the human brain, emphasising the limbic system underneath the twin-hemisphered cortex and above the brain stem.

Diagram 4 shows a view of the brain that emphasizes the highly complex and modular limbic system. This is tucked under the cortex and is fairly close to the cerebellum (see diagram 3). Evolutionary biologists believe that the lymbic system, which focuses upon instincts and emotions, rather than thinking, developed from an ancient pre-mammalian brain near the top of the spinal chord. This limbic system, that looks like nothing else on earth, though some of its grayish modules appear as being a little like grapes, is clearly present beneath a then very tiny cortex at as little as 14 weeks of fetal gestation. Since this system is the response and control centre for our emotional life, we make a very early start as emotional beings. Our thinking brain parts are relatively delayed in their development.

The broad functions of most of the labeled parts of diagrams 3 and 4, including the limbic system, are indicated in table 5 below.

Table 5: Some brain components and their prime functions

Brain component	Main function
Corpus callosum	Shunts information between left and right lobes
Parietal lobes (mid cortex)	Movement, spatial orientation, calculation
Cerebellum (close to stem)	Ancient small brain governing motor coordination
Occipital lobes	Visual processing at rear part of cortical lobes
Brain stem	Body-brain information, conduit via spinal chord
Lymbic system (see below)	Complex of modules, electrically very potent and densely connected upwards to the cortex
Temporal lobes	Sound, speech comprehension, spiritual sensing
Frontal lobes	Thinking, conceptualizing, planning, as well as the storage of emotional memories
Limbic system component*	**Basic function**
Amygdala	Emotional centre and alarm system (e.g. for fear)
Hypothalmus	Adjusts body to keep it adapted to environment**
Pineal gland*	An endocrine gland helping to control hormones
Thalamus	Relay station, redirecting incoming information
Hippocampus	Long-term memory connector

* Only one of these; two of the remainder.
** Shared with the pituitary gland

The two halves of the neo-cortex are 'driven', circuit-wise, by the relatively small *right and left* sub-cortical primal emotive centre, the *amygdala*. Some such organ is present in the relatively small-for-body-weight reptilian brains of species such as dinosaurs and lizards. The whole, two-halved limbic system (diagram 4) operates as a high-density centre of electrical activity, registers and distributes signals from the surrounding environment, prompting responses with or without conscious thought processing. The left and right emotional centre, the *amygdala*, as part of the limbic system, is crucial in this functioning.

Many more neural fibers project from the *amygdala* to the rational-logical cortex than in the reverse direction. Centrally, this means that we need to recognize that *our emotions and their monitoring and management are central to enhancing both our physical-manipulative skills and our intellectual functions.* That is why it is proper for us to refer to 'the emotional brain-mind', rather than to view emotions as a kind of extra to rational thinking and acting. *Emotions* generated in the limbic system, and impacted by a range of hormonal activities elsewhere in the body, *are thus our most basic of brain reactions.*

3.5 Managing the emotional centre

It should now be clear that we inhabit much more a universe of feelings than of machinery. In a real sense our thoughts are intellectually processed feelings and emotions. Unsurprisingly, if our mood or emotional state is low or stressed, no matter what the cause, our thinking and acting are likely to be less efficient or impaired.

Diagram 5 shows, with huge simplification, how emotional information is sent to the conscious brain and the *amygdala* by two routes. The path to the latter is relatively short, so that our emotional reactions are significantly faster than our conscious ones. The safe, wise and optimum management of emotional reactions therefore often needs to build in *reflective pause-time* so as to allow for the incorporation of our thinking processes.

Diagram 5: **Schematic Brain Diagram For Emotional Processing**

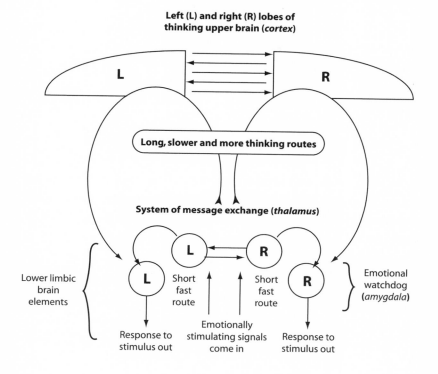

**Left (L) and right (R) lobes of
thinking upper brain (*cortex*)**

Notes concerning Diagram 5

1. Almost all components of the limbic and cortical brain double up as left (L) and right R) elements, with various cross-links.

2. Both limbic and cortical areas of the brain have many sub-components, details of whose function, outlined in table 5, are still being explored and mapped by neuroscientists.

3. The diagram is indicative of what needs to happen in managing downsides of emotion; namely, we must learn to reflect and encourage the development of the long and slower message routes involving the cortex. This demands

effort, especially if the disciplines of reflection are not taught early in life.

4. The twined (right and left sided) a*mygdala* is in essence the brain's alarm and response centre, originally evolved in the animal kingdom to aid survival. If different parts of the *amygdala* are stimulated, different emotions intensify, such as fear, anger, or a sense of warm comfort and safety (akin to joy).

In the light of diagram 5 and the notes accompanying, if we are presented with a threat, such as a double-decker bus bearing down on us, the *amygdala* will instantaneously trigger the action brain to move us out of the way fast, that is to flee the threat. If the moving object on wheels is less threatening, for example a child's pushchair, the adult response will be to 'fight' it, to becalm it, and so eliminate its potential danger. If we meet a bully, whether on a committee, or the boss at work, or in the school playground, or in a family context, wisely even if not especially consciously, we will evaluate, for our own preservation, whether to withdraw (flight), confront (fight), or play at least temporarily a 'cool' tactic (appease). These three possibilities to the bully stress might be expressed as 'jump back', 'lunge forward', or 'smile nicely', and essentially pass the next move over to the bully who, likely as not, is far more used to an instant response.

Sometimes of course a flight or fight response, or a continuous appeasement of someone's behavior, may make the consequences more catastrophic than the original threat. Many times we have all acted in situations of threat and made matters worse. It is therefore very important that most emotional responses generated by the ancient-evolved *amygdala* are mediated by the thinking cortical part of the brain; that is, through the longer and slower route shown in Diagram 5. This habit is not natural, and needs patiently acquired learning

Personal Exercise 6

Write short notes about an actual incident, or a series of connected incidents in which you were or are in effect faced with the 'flight, fight or appease' options. From the unpressured time perspective that you now enjoy as you calmly think about this, review what you did, or have been planning to do, and evaluate your actions. What do you think you have learned about yourself from this reflection?

Monitoring, controlling and actively managing our emotions is in effect the reverse of the processes required to feel them. The a*mygdalas'* fast, almost instantaneous automatic response route prompting body arousal is followed about a quarter of a second later by information processing in the frontal lobes of the cortex. This will either confirm the instantaneous bodily response (such as getting out of the way of a moving bus), or prompt a change in response by sending a calming down message to parts of the limbic system. Through this means, emotions that could be damaging if expressed forcefully in the context, are held in check, most of the time at least. When strong emotions are not in check, emotional control breaks down; as we say, 'we lose it', perhaps for a range of reasons, some of which may go a long way back in our lives.

For example, if the signals sent from the cortex to the limbic system are too weak or insufficiently focused to over-ride the *amygdala*, we may expect trouble. This happens, mostly quite normally, in young children during familiar temper tantrums, when they may, for example, throw their toys around. Children's brains are essentially immature and unbalanced, their cortical and neural network development being no match for the 'calls' of their *amygdalas* that are more or less fully mature at birth. Time alone may not enable this phase to be shunned, and some adults, even holding responsible positions, can be seen to view such infantile tantrums as a child's means of getting its own way. Perhaps you know of someone like that, or can admit some such trait in yourself?

Wise parents enhance emotional and cortical maturity by forms of careful social control (that is, discipline). This neither over-reacts to nor ignores antisocial behaviour, such as tantrums. In so doing parents are helping new brain circuits to form and then to get exercised in the youngster. Children who are rarely encouraged to activate the potential cortical control of their emotions may become poorly controlled as adults, the relevant brain circuits having been under-nourished during crucial stages of development.

Damage to the neural pathways from the limbic system to the cortex, or to the cortex or limbic system directly, may impair the desirable inhibition of the *amygdala's* first intuition. In contrast, it seems that some with psychopathic tendencies have under-active *amygdalas*, so that they do not feel intense emotion, and are therefore lacking in remorse or fear of punishment when they step harshly upon others' toes. A controlled study in Oxford in 1996 found that nearly one sixth of UK managers fulfilled the diagnostic criteria for psychopathology, officially known as 'anti-social personality disorder'.

A weak ability to sense emotion in others, which in essence means being able to 'get out of the self and into others' shoes', seems most likely to have its origins in insecure early bonding. Close and rewarding interaction between infants and particularly their mothers (referred to in section 2.4), seems necessary to stimulate and maintain the normal function of the *amygdala*, and much other sense perception. As noted earlier there are tremendous preventative social policy implications arising from such findings that are now well-researched.

Brain mapping, now becoming sophisticated through various types of brain scans, seems likely to be of help in the future to enable improved recovery for stroke, head accident and psychiatric patients. Some criminals with poor impulse control and/or sense of others' feelings may also thereby be assisted to achieve more fulfilled lives.

Now we move on to aspects of the human brain as a complex and delicate living chemical factory.

3.6 The brain's chemical sensitivity

Chemicals are understandably pivotal to both the electrical functions of brain cells and the transmitting and connecting structures between them. Our genes are important in brain formation and function from conception onwards, but chemicals present in the bloodstream also play an important role. For example, we now know that the placenta does not have the capability to filter all the toxins that may be present in the mother's circulation; these include alcohol and nicotine as well as, for example, the AIDS virus. Thus, inappropriate drug taking during pregnancy is known to impact babies' blood and brain chemistry, including the tragedy of rendering some of them effectively addicted at birth. Natural opiates for example are highly specific, operating with exquisite precision, like keys to locks, at a few transmitter-receptor synaptic sites. Morphine and certain other drugs tend to provide an imperfect fit, posing as natural chemicals but blocking receptors, and so fouling natural brain circuits in-the-making.

Some drugs, including alcohol, when regularly taken beyond the womb, tend to flood sites for the growth of connecting synapses. Cumulatively these may literally marinade or 'pickle' the brain. Connecting receptor sites for circuit building (see diagram 2, page 56) are thereby rendered less sensitive, and this causes drug doses to rise to achieve the same effect. So addiction emerges. Natural personality and sociability may then literally go down the plughole by brain damage, impairing civic functions and causing huge relational distress.

Of course with supportive skill and continual personal determination, addictions, having changed brain structure and function, can be held at bay, and often permanently. But as every recovered alcoholic or other type of addict knows, there is no absolute cure, only day-by-day discipline, for their brains have become super-sensitive to the addictive chemical or cocktail that they had been using.

The brain, as driver of the central nervous system, has its chemistry modified for a period of time whenever we take a painkiller, such as aspirin, or mood changing drug such as a tranquillizer or an anti-depressant. For example, antidepressants work on neurotransmitter levels mainly through enhancing a substance called serotonin, which when low in concentration seems to enhance anger levels and thence depression.

Manipulating brain chemistry is the way that most psychiatric therapies work, but there are always risks of addiction or other side effects. At least in the short-term, drug therapies tend to have more impact than the 'talk therapies' of various schools of counseling. For its clients, skilled counseling endeavors to trigger fresh and more helpful brain circuits into action at emotional-rational interfaces by sensitive reflective discourse. This encourages modifications in personal perceptions of reality, thus building confidence concerning capacities to change, even in small areas of life, rather than feel or become simply a victim of circumstance. At almost any stage of life, counseling and spiritual guidance can prompt fresh willpower to change personal outlook and behavior, not least when stressed.

3.7 Living with respect for the grain of the brain

Our brains carry the evidence of both nurture and neglect, but because of the huge untapped potential of all our brains, in which few ever use more than about 40 per cent of their neural capacity, there is truth in the old saying that we are never too old to learn if we are not too stubborn. We need to cooperate with our endowed neural equipment and 'go with the grain of our brain'. This is not only a personal but also an institutional challenge. Many of our social organizations (workplaces, schools, clubs and churches, for example), comprising combinations of individual people, past and present, are not managed in a brain friendly manner. Probably the biggest cause of organizational inefficiency rests in failures to create climates that draw out positive psychic energies amongst those involved.

With age, our neural modifications and extensions may take more intense effort, for not only is there some atrophy within brain circuits but also a net loss of neurons, an estimated one per second, making some 30 million out of 100 million in a lifetime. We know for example that learning a second language is easier when brains are immersed in bilingualism in childhood. Nonetheless, focused effort, that is 'willing' rather than 'feeling', may call into play spare neural capacity where it becomes needed. My mother, for example, at 90 years of age, recovered much of her ability to write with her right hand after a right-sided stroke had completely demolished that skill. Through her persistence with allocated physiotherapy exercises, working almost exclusively on her weak side, she was able to trigger alternative brain circuits into action, measurable compensating for those deadened by the stroke.

Having outlined something of the brain's basic character, including the centrality of its emotional disposition, we need to recognize a few basic consequences. Although the adult brain is only about 2 per cent of our body weight, it continues to commandeer some 20 per cent of available body energy. If we are to be rational as we plan social and personal life, we should become more conscious of befriending our brains, moving with 'the grain of the brain'. In part that means giving full recognition to our basic human needs as outlined in section 2.2.

Hence, aside from avoiding those bloodstream drugs that literally 'blow' the mind and eventually reduce its bounce-back capability, there is our human need for:

- continuing *encouragement* and involvement in worthwhile activities, through which our brains are 'impressed', so learning to exercise insightful and considerate judgment
- continuing *stimulation* and interaction, through which we

learn to express ourselves and the variety of our character

- continuing personal *reflection*, through which, given our uniquely large cortex, we are able to review events and, if need be, change our attitude and approach to our social and physical environment, and
- continuing participation in *creative tasks*, through which we can prompt or feed new 'intuitive' brain connections, and thus make new impressions upon our physical and social world.

These features, when embedded in an atmosphere of sensitivity, thoughtfulness and 'mutual mind-reading', which is of the nature of secure love, allow the whole personality, emotional-brain driven, to flower.

Humans, in relation to the rest of the animal kingdom, have relatively large brains in relation to their body mass. We also have a prolonged infancy and dependency period over which there are amazing natural possibilities for learning, provided that environments are and remain 'brain-friendly'. However, all of us may regress in emotionally harsh climates, and table 6 summarizes some relevant comparisons.

Table 6: Environments, friendly or otherwise, for human brains

'Brain-friendly' factors	'Brain-unfriendly' factors
A secure and stimulating environment	Insecure prompts and excessive stimulation
Questioning and curiosity encouraged	Blind, unquestioning obedience to authority
A sound and balanced diet	Drug and alcohol abuse
An easy birth	A prolonged and difficult birth
Time for relaxation and regular sleep	Long-term rush, pressure and irregular hours
Reliable and good-hearted company	Social exclusion and isolation
Praise and encouragement	Harsh criticism and discouragement

A balanced, secure, or indeed wise mind is developed and richly interconnected in both of its hemispheres. Behavior: what people actually do and the way they act, is the product of the interactions between the left and right sides of the brain, primed by the limbic system, and executed through the central nervous system. Hence the recognition, acceptance, understanding and management of feelings and emotions is a central task of life, and, as stated in chapter 1, a hugely neglected element in formal education.

Modern neuroscience is clearly confirming that social and emotional 'intelligences' are vitally important. It is changing our views of consciousness, and of some limits to our free will. It is suggesting that internal evaluations of the self (our inner self-concept and self-esteem) are more important than external grades or other tokens of performance, which if intensively demanded can be harmful to a good sense of self and our abilities to collaborate.

Neuroscience is also suggesting that in a responsibly free society all citizens need to acquire a greater sense of internal control and guidance capacities than to rely too much upon external controls or indoctrination, however subtle. Another way of phrasing that is to say that the core function of basic nurture and education should be personal and responsible empowerment. Tackling chronic social stressors impacting the development of neural systems among the young that regulate learning, motivation, morals and memory becomes imperative for social policy, and, as noted, has clear implications for maternal well-being and family mutual support in community contexts. Each of us is a complex mix of our genes, and our social history over far more than one generation. Going with 'the grain of the brain' by acting upon the basic principles summarized in Table 6 involves taking due care to ensure that our personal and social environments are warm, stimulating, reliable, reflective, sensitive and encouraging.

Personal Exercise 7

In the light of some of the facts presented in this chapter about the human brain, record your feelings now about your own brain and its evolution to this point. Record one or two practical steps that you can reasonably take to look after your brain, thus moving to a more brain-friendly lifestyle.

3.8 Wisdom and smart brain behavior?

It remains an open question as to whether we are wise enough to take the emerging evidence of our human neuro-biological and socio-ecological nature seriously, and on a global scale. Some of the pace of contemporary social change is far from brain-friendly when viewed in an evolutionary and historical perspective. Much ancient wisdom, concerning time for inner reflection, for example, we ignore, as if each generation must, now with increasingly blinkered and costly arrogance, re-invent what our forebears had slowly and often painfully discovered. Clearly a modern university education does not make one wise!

The search for personal meaning and purpose and a good life is the main function of the mind. Now, our 'wising-up', perhaps more than ever before, depends upon taking our full human nature seriously. Properly illuminated by the relevant evidence now amassed, this demands something of an educational, social and economic revolution in which a materialism of 'enough' must replace that of insatiable greed. But you and I as individuals, and in our most immediate social networks, cannot, and need not wait for that revolution. For no matter what has gone before in our lives by way of both terrible and noble events, *we can all make a difference* to the quality of our emotional lives, and at least those of others close by.

From this chapter, the important issue for us to recognize is that our emotions are deeply embedded in brain activity, and that in important respects they 'drive' our thinking minds and responsive bodies. Likewise, these same emotions are impacted by misconceived thinking such as false beliefs about what we perceive as our 'reality', through which unhelpful brain circuits can play real tricks on us. Our emotions are also affected by offensive actions, including bodily abuse through time-pressed and drugged, antagonistic lifestyles. Our emotions are therefore a real part of us, and may not be displaced, though they may be consciously or subconsciously buried; and these emotions, as we will see in chapter 5, have both innate and adaptable qualities.

Here we have covered the most relevant 'basic lay science' that is the backcloth for greater emotional mastery. Table 7 gives, by way of some revision, and a little extension concerning the significance of the prefrontal lobes and the heart's electromagnetism, a summary of our evolved basic heart-brain system as five interdependent neural structures linked to function and eras of phased development from conception in the womb.

Table 7: The Evolved Heart Brain: A Basis for Smart Behavior

Neural structure	Function	Development
1. *Reptilian* action centre at the top of the spinal chord	Survival sensory-motor habit; fear defense systems	Significantly in the *first* trimester of fetal growth
2. *Old mammalian* limbic system (fed by immune system)	Emotional sensing within relationship; now and then	Forming from the *second* trimester; needs taming
3. *New mammalian* neo-cortex above limbic area; 80% of cranial cavity space	Thinking-language, linked to and driven by feeling and sense of futures	Forming from the *third* trimester to about age 12, needing balanced education
4. *Prefrontal lobes* (forebrain-hindbrain circuits with central nervous system)	Creativity, fresh perception and imagination. Deals with energy flows	None pre-birth; spurts in toddler phase, and age 15–21; options of inner war or peace
5. *Thinking* and *intelligent heart* radiating its own special signals	Neurotransmitter and receiver; far more than simply a blood pump	Nature's continual call: a resonance of the social heart with best brain waves

Recent research suggests that the prefrontal lobes, linked to the hindbrain, by a latent potential spurt in mid to late adolescence, may be an advanced theatre for human development.

It is helpful, but not enough, for us to know of this material concerning heart-brain functions. We need to set such knowledge in a range of contexts of our own experience, and outlook, so that we can in practice get a better and more rewarding grip on our inner and outer lives. This does not mean denying or suppressing our emotions, far from it, for those routes are bedeviled with postponed problems, some of which may become acute or severe. For example, an outwardly angry young man's emotional difficulties are at least visible, whereas a quietly angry, isolated, repressed loner is often a civic tragedy waiting to happen.

Much of the rest of this book is therefore devoted to gaining further insights and avenues through which we may get a more helpful grip on and balance to our brain-heart emotional and relational lives. Awaiting there is possibly another phase of human evolution.

4
LANGUAGE IN EDUCATING OUR EMOTIONS

4
LANGUAGE IN EDUCATING OUR EMOTIONS

'The limits of my language stand for the limits of my world.'
Wittgenstein, 1889-1951

'The secret of our emotions never lies in the bare object,
but in its subtle relations to our own past.'
George Eliot, 1819-80, in *Romola*

In chapter 2 we noted the extensive links between our emotions and our different types of relationships. Some focus was given to this through the interwoven concepts of relational and emotional intelligence, now illuminated by neuroscience.

Both our understanding and the expression of our emotions are major aspects in the vitally important arena of human communication. Socially inadequate expression of our own emotions, or impoverished understanding of others' emotions, both tend to create climates for interpersonal misunderstandings. Involved in these are likely to be senses of frustration, discomfort, distrust, withdrawal, stubborn attitudes and awkward or disruptive behavior.

This chapter (and its cluster of exercises) is concerned with improving language use for *feelings* and *emotions*. Included is a working distinction between these two common words that tend to be used interchangeably. Getting some of our language clear is a first step in marshalling our thinking about our feeling, and, no less, our feeling about our thinking.

4.1 Defining feelings, emotions and mood

Interestingly, the English language has only about fifty words through which feeling states are expressed. At the other extreme, Sanskrit, the most logical of all world languages, has about nine hundred such words. This rather limited vocabulary is arguably a handicap for most English mother tongue speakers.

For example, most of us can reasonably imagine a feeling of acceptance by, and consequent belonging to, another person or group. This is a generalized example of a sense of secure attachment discussed in section 2.4; that sense of comfort in being totally accepted by specific others. But this excellent feeling requires at least several words or a sentence in English to describe, let alone explain. However, in Japanese there is just one word for this comfortable sense of solidarity, *amae*. This word is apparently derived from the original Chinese ideogram for the safe suckling of infants at mother's breast, conveying a sense of fusion and oneness. Perhaps it is no cultural accident that post-industrial rampant individualism and social atomization, now evident in English-speaking nations, caught on so swiftly with us. Do we simply lack enough simple words for the most important things concerning our human welfare? Is it left too much to the skilled poet or dramatist in English to conjure up expressive sensitivities not present in our cultural mainstreams?

Dictionaries suggest several associations for the verb 'to feel'. For example:

- touch sensation, as in 'this wood feels rough'
- physical condition, as in 'I feel hot'
- to have a wish or a preference for, as in 'I feel like having a shower'
- to proceed cautiously, as in 'I am feeling my way up the passage'
- to sympathize or empathize with someone, as in 'I feel for that distressed mother'.

Perhaps more particularly for our purpose here:

- to be conscious of or affected by an emotion, and
- to have a vague emotional impression.

For clarity, I here define *feelings* as '*emotional susceptibilities*', or as '*expressive of emotions*', thus giving logical precedence to the word 'emotion'. However, English dictionaries are not particularly helpful in defining emotion. For example, the Oxford Reference Dictionary simply says of emotions: 'strong mental or instinctive feelings, such as love or fear'; this is not simply brief, but, as we shall see in this and the next two chapters, limiting and even confusing.

At this point, the following statements of comparison and interaction are intended to help to clarify these two terms. In the next chapter, the presence of only *six innate emotions* within the human species will be proposed within a simple model that helps us to find our way through the potential jungle of feelings and emotions language.

Let us agree, here at least, to view emotions as rather more fundamental, and perhaps less transient, than feelings. In this way we can view feelings as particular manifestations of a deeper emotion, rather than the other way round. In other words we can think of an emotion as 'a strong or intense feeling', or as 'sets of associated feelings', reflecting their natural interplay. In addition, as we shall also see in more detail in the next chapter, some emotions may be labeled, according to circumstance and particularly if expressed, as having some ethical character. So, for example anger, even 'righteous anger', may, according to its context and expression, be viewed as good and constructive, or bad and destructive. In contrast, we might agree that *our feelings just are feelings,* neither right nor wrong. So we can make a clear distinction between feeling angry, being angry, and being out of control with anger.

While addressing matters of definition, a further associated word is 'mood', that dictionaries tend to call 'a state of mind'. Alongside this term is 'moody', a character trait that we tend to associate with those whose moods are variable and unpredictable. For example, over raising a problem with a moody person, we might advise a friend to choose a time when you can catch that person in a good mood.

The literature suggests that whereas a basic emotion such as joy might last for a few seconds, or at most a minute or two, a happy mood is likely to last much longer from several minutes to a few hours. For example, our favorite football team scoring a goal triggers moments of joy; the team gaining a win result can make us happy for the rest of the day. Moods seem present in us for relatively long periods of time. A great meal or concert can help mood; a particular tang or taste, or orchestral chord is more a trigger of emotion. A low or depressed mood might last for days, and not seem unrelated to any one issue in particular. One way of articulating the differences here is to view mood as a consistent extension of emotion, and its associated feelings, over time.

In addition, types of mood are basically only classified in lay language as extremes around some kind of neutral, ordinary, mundane average. The contrasting extremes might be described as dark/light, low/high, bad/good, depressed/elated, negative/positive, and so on, but they all amount to roughly the same thing. Of course emotions and feelings in their variety are present within mood, but they are sharper in expressiveness. Moreover certain drugs acting as brain-sensitive chemicals, whether used within supervised therapy, or for so-called 'recreation', can change mood, sometimes markedly, and for at least several hours. However, drugs do not basically change the range of emotions and feelings that make up the spectrum of mood. Hence it is perhaps more helpful to speak therapeutically of mood disorders than of emotional disorders, and since this is more a text of self-help than therapy, mood will now only rarely be referred to.

Personal Exercise 8

Make a list of feelings and emotions that are likely to arise in you in each of the following circumstances:

1. A policeman walking along your street.
2. A contented baby in a pram.
3. An ambulance on an emergency call.
4. Wearing a new pair of shoes.
5. Christmas Day.
6. Losing at cards or at a board game.
7. Being deliberately mislead.
8. Untidy personal belongings at home.
9. The boss saying 'Well done'.
10. A nearby crying baby on a bus or train.
11. Litter in the countryside.
12. Someone is depending on you.
13. Meeting a stranger.
14. Giving someone a gift.
15. Receiving a gift.
16. Loud noises from next door.

Now, in the light of the text so far in this chapter, circle those words you have recorded for these sixteen items that you think might be best labeled 'emotions', rather than feelings. (Remember that there are no right or wrong answers here. The exercise simply aims to improve a reflective familiarity with elements of your emotional life.)

Next, record in your own words any emotional dilemmas or difficulties that any of the sample situations prompt in you, such as a feeling or emotion that hinted of pain or distress, or which you associate with an unhelpful negativity. This might suggest avenues for your personal growth as you move through the rest of the text.

4.2 Human imagination

One way for us to access and extend our awareness of the range of our feelings and emotions is through activating our imagination. Our human imagination is like an antenna projected from the known into part mystery and speculation. Good stories, novels or poetry, sometimes music, drama and other expressive arts, can aid our imagination, whether as consumers or producers. So also may 'fantasy journeys' in which we agree to take an imaginary 'trip' in our mind's eye on our own, or under guidance from a leader. Engaging in Exercise 8 above, for example, required some inner imagination, from past clues or memories.

Young children tend to have rich imaginations, partly because they are less self-conscious about fantasy. In an apparently fact-laden and beguilingly science-driven world, it is sometimes hard for adults to give freedom to their imaginations. However, all works of art, and most scientific and mathematical breakthroughs are the part-product of imagination, speculation and hypothesis building through 'what-if' speculations.

Almost everyone has 'what-if' thoughts, some relatively impersonal relating to the inanimate world, but many are rich in emotional content, such as those embodying anxiety or of wild fantasy. Next is a composite imaginative poem drawn from several thirteen-year-olds' 'what-ifs', produced in the context of a class-teacher's assignment. The lines are rich in fantasy and give insight into a range of emotions, particularly rational and irrational fears, several at least being possibly quite close to these youngsters' lives and natures at the time.

> ***Just Imagine: What Ifs?***
> (Edited; courtesy of the Steiner School, Auckland, New Zealand, June 1999)
>
> Last night while I lay in the gloom
> Some 'what ifs' crawled into my room,
> And pranced and partied through the night
> Direct into my ear with great delight.

What if I can't get out of bed?
What if a book lands on my head?
What if my brother is nice to me?
What if I could no thing see?
What if roses did not grow?
What if the sun did not glow?
What if skyscrapers covered the earth?
What if I had never come to birth?
What if oranges were blue?
What if I never knew what to do?
What if fire did not burn?
What if I could never learn?
What if I did not try in school?
What if I broke just every rule?
What if the sea did not touch the shore?
And what if I was extremely poor?
What if aliens invade our land?
And then they take the seaside sand?
What if my parents disappeared?
What if Dad started to grow a beard?
What if I was a cheetah?
What if I became a cheater?

What if this poem never came to an end?
Then what a dreadful life I'd spend
Entrapped in this same 'what if' trance,
Doing that same old 'what if' dance.
For mostly everything goes quite swell,
Until those 'what ifs' start their hell.

Personal Exercise 9

Write down two or three examples of 'what-ifs' that tend to recur in your own life as you 'just imagine'. What do they seem to say about both your emotional disposition, and possible beliefs that perhaps feed these speculative emotional trends?

4.3 Beyond words: the visual element

Our available 'language' for feelings and emotions is not only verbal. Humans have other avenues, so-called 'non-verbal languages', through which we 'speak' without actually talking or writing words. These include gestures, facial expressions, body posture, clothing and other matters of physical appearance, with a wide spectrum of possibilities according to gender, age, culture and social class background.

We may easily misread a person's character and emotional life through these outward appearances, for not many people 'wear their hearts on their sleeve'. For example, nuns and monks have angers and fears similar to the rest of us, and from time to time these exacerbate their supposedly holy living in convent and monastery communities. Likewise, 'a stiff upper lip' is said to be a frequent trait of the English that covers up shock and pain. Some suggest that the appearance of the eyes can be a window into someone's soul-space; hence those who never 'look another in the eye' are likely to be in some form of emotional or ethically related hiding, a form of cover-up.

Personal exercise 10

- *Look at photographs involving facial expressions and/or gestures of people in a recent newspaper, magazine or in a family photograph album. What do you think that the various subjects*

> *in the photos are feeling? Speculate about the accuracy of your suggestions, and maybe test the reliability of your perception with a friend.*
>
> • *Is there a particular emotion that you personally probably tend to hide through the way you appear or speak? If so, under what kinds of circumstance does this tend to happen? Again, you might also check this out with a close friend.*

Many blind people seem to develop a sensitive sense of emotional atmosphere without either directly emoting words or visual clues. This also tends to happen to people who have lived together for a long time. For example, I can certainly sense when my wife of over forty years is troubled about something, without her either speaking or looking at me. Without such long experience of atmospheres within a particular relationship it would be surprising, as well as very disconcerting, if most people could not improve, and short-cut, their 'reading' of others' emotions. That quality is most important in being able to be empathetic, and to imagine what it is like to be in others' situational 'shoes'. As we will see in the next two chapters, there are shared frameworks to help us to mould more sensitive responses.

4.4 Trawling emotional origins

In the last chapter we examined the evolutionary history, anatomy and physiology of humans' emotional and feeling life. Now, through examples and exercises, some of the possible biographical elements contributing to our present experiences of emotional life are explored.

In some sense our memory is basically the retained and embedded feeling of past feelings, for occasions of strong emotion tend to etch events in our deep memory. I can, for example remember details of what happened on the day that my late father had his first heart attack in 1966, coinciding with the first day in my new job as a university lecturer in Cambridge; also of the day some sixteen years later when one son, then aged twelve, had his leg broken in a school rugby game.

Here, the reflective exercises serve to probe, or even excavate, aspects of our emotional formation, and to give practice in finding and using appropriate descriptive language for feelings.

Memorable events in childhood may be short-lived, and though to our adult eyes may seem quite trivial, their impact upon personal development, particularly emotional reactions, could be profound and have long-term consequences. For example, a man aged 35 reports:

> 'Not long before my second birthday I was sitting in my push chair, apparently outside a shop, when a large black Labrador dog suddenly came from around the back and started to lick my face. I screamed and cried a lot. Mum dashed out of the shop to comfort me, and I have been basically scared of most dogs ever since. I always try to cross the road if I see a dog coming.'

Personal exercise 11

Record, conveniently in tabular form as shown, four separate situations remembered from your childhood (and before the age of about 14), when you experienced the four kinds of feelings indicated. Complete, if possible, all the table cells.

MEMORY OF SOME EARLY EMOTIONAL EXPERIENCES

Emotion Situation facts	Happy and joyous 1	Sad, even depressed 2	Scared and fearful 3	Cross, angry, even raging 4
My aproximate age at the time (years)				
What happened at the time, including the people involved.				
What happened afterwards?				
Any paricular consequences now?				

4.5 Feelings and values

Section 2.5 noted the interactive two-way link between emotions and personal values. Our values tend to shape the character of many of our emotional responses, whether at the extremes of joy or of angry disapproval. Within some of our emotional pains from poor past experiences lie origins of at least some of our strongly held values.

For example, someone who often felt abandoned when having to wait for a loved-one as a child may become fastidious about punctuality, and highly intolerant and unforgiving of others who keep them waiting. Another person, experiencing as a youngster the negative consequences of poor money management, may become particularly frugal in their approach to household budgeting, and highly sensitive to, or even angered by 'waste', including all forms of alcoholic drink and gambling. Past emotional pain can echo subconsciously within even very fine values held in the present.

The use of time and money, both being subject to personal discretion and practical limits, usually say a great deal about people's living values. A high proportion of household tensions arise from time and money 'mismanagement'. In turn these tend to trigger further hassles through emotional mismanagement, the deeper origins of the present tensions rarely surfacing to be dealt with by calm and comfortable communication. Strong feelings that may seem to be someone's direct fault or causation amid the pressures of now, often lie in much earlier forgotten or suppressed biography.

Prejudices, which in fact reflect strong hostile feelings, are a source of defensive emotions and behavior, particularly in response to both rational and exaggerated fears. Table 8 gives four examples.

Table 8: Values, feelings and likely behavior consequences

Value held	Some feelings associated	Resulting attitudes and behavior
Child safety	Fear, disgust, shame, anger	Distrust of strangers; over-protective
Competitive success	Striving, doubt, aggression	Driven lifestyles; rejection of failure
Bodily beauty	Pride, self-doubt, rejection	Narrowed perceptions; fear of aging
Punctuality	Anxiety, time stress, anger	Plan far ahead; rigidity, intolerance

Prejudices of a racial, religious and physical nature are very common. Negative emotional reactions to others are often based upon both ignorance and a sense of group-related threat to personal fortunes, rather than balanced evidence and insight. Crowds can develop collective emotions of their own, this sometimes happens quite quickly from herd instincts (see further in section 10.4).

Personal exercise 12

Select two advertisements from a glossy magazine, one that you like, and one that you dislike. Record the feelings and emotions that each advert evokes within you. Do any of the emotions roused seem related to your upbringing at home, whether by way of reinforcement or active rejection of the implicit values that you experienced? Endeavor to name the values visible or underlying the messages contained in the advertisements that you selected.

4.6 Feelings concerning attachment, separation and loss

A common and crucial area around which much of our emotional life is centered concerns our strong human bonds, or those that we long to become strong and fulfilling. These are relationships that we experience, or hope to experience, as reliable and meaningful, particularly attachments to our loved ones, but also our bonds to special, loved objects, as noted in section 2.4. Concerning the latter, damage to or the total loss of a valued object, precious to a person (even if it does not have a high monetary value), generally prompts a range of disturbing feelings and emotions. In this area, the total loss of one's home, workshop or office and contents through fire would be extreme examples.

When we have become attached to someone, or something, we are implicitly committed to their or its welfare and safety. We greatly value the person or object of our commitment, almost as if this were part of us. In fact our key attachments become a part of our identity, our 'story' and of how we define and describe ourselves in relation. Hence, strong emotions are very natural if an attachment's welfare is threatened, and a sense of devastation and deep grief are the natural responses to a total loss through a death or through the prospect of or actual severance of relationship.

Terminal losses are fortunately relatively rare over the life course, though everyone is virtually guaranteed at least a few, including one's own death, the approach of which is extensively an emotional matter, even given the comforts of a religious faith in an afterlife. Some, through misfortune, may have to cope with a number of terminal losses close together. In such cases, grief is compounded and the phases of the natural processes of bereavement (usually about eighteen months for a close relative) may become extended.

There are however many less severe but significant 'losses' associated with normal changes over the life course. Examples of these are when the time comes to leave school, or to change jobs, maybe moving from a house or district in which there have been good memories; loss of job through redundancy or retirement, or, more mundanely, selling a car which has served well, having to give up a favorite food for health reasons, or reaching another decade in age milestones. Table 3, page 42 listed some common feelings associated with loss, contrasted with those of secure attachment.

Not all 'leavings behind' are losses invoking grief or sadness. There can be many positive aspects to healthy separations, particularly those involving life transitions, such as leaving home in a mature manner or taking up a new job. Relationships are rarely static, and sometimes we need to move on through life stages such as those outlined in Table 4, page 51. A good separation will not resent the past, but will be able to launch aspects of new life from the foundations of what went before. Where those foundations have been too shaky, particularly emotionally, then separation may embody some healthy escape. For example, some people are very relieved when they leave home or school, or change jobs, especially if they have felt improper constriction and insensitivity, even rejection, from key carers, teachers or supervisors.

As noted in section 2.4, one of the paradoxes of attachment and separation processes is that healthy attachments are not 'clingy', infringing or engulfing. A secure attachment is more a flexible and reciprocal dynamic bond, rather than one of well-set cement. From about one to two years of age a healthy attachment can both endure a separation (initially quite short) and experience a joy at the return of the nurturing loved one. This demonstrates a growing sense of trust. Insecure attachments, felt as untrustworthy, either prompt panic on separation, or later indifference (in extreme cases even fear) when the loved and 'theoretically' nurturing figure returns.

A handful of secure attachments are vital to our emotional and wider well being from cradle to grave. Without them we may literally be 'lost souls'. Yet, paradoxically, with them we are bound some day to experience loss and grief. If we never give our hearts, our commitment, to at least a few people and projects, we are likely to live a life of disillusion and loneliness. This is much less bearable than the experience of loss when a good project is concluded, or a close friend or relative, to whom we have not clung unhealthily, leaves our soul-space. Yet, as we will see when we give further consideration to the subject of love in chapter 7, it is very difficult, if not impossible, for us to give our hearts, and make emotional commitments if we have not first experienced reliable commitment and love as a gift from someone else.

Personal exercise 13

Choose two or three of the following six examples of loss that apply within your biography. For each chosen example outline the associated strong feelings you remember at the time, and now. It may help to use a tabular record of the kind shown.

- Loss of a favorite possession (e.g. a piece of jewelry).
- Death of a close friend or relative (name the person in your notes).
- Being made redundant at work.
- Moving from your favorite house.
- Being 'dropped' by your first serious boy or girl friend.
- A thwarted, but realistic ambition.

Outline of loss example (and year date)	Strong feelings		Coping mode	Change now
	then	now		
1.				
2.				
3.				

Reflect upon and note how you coped with each chosen loss at the time (e.g. faced, denied, buried, laughed at it). Note any particular help that you experienced over these losses, and in what ways, if any, have the selected losses changed you now.

Finally, write a note about how you view your own capacity to empathize with others' losses?

4.7 Feelings expressed through the creative arts

Down the ages the creative arts have often been avenues of expressing emotions. Sometimes these varied media involve mainly words, as in poetry, novels and drama, but more frequently the emotions are expressed figuratively, as in dance (including ballet), sculpture, pottery, textiles, painting and music.

Here is not the place to analyze these varied art forms. Rather we simply need to note their aesthetic and feelings-invoking importance in all cultures. As symbolic and practical expression these may convey very personal meanings, transmitted from artists as creators and performers who evoke deep emotions within their audiences.

Personal exercise 14

Select one of your favorite poems, paintings, pieces of music or other artworks. Briefly record your feelings about this piece of art, endeavoring to record how this seems to resonate with your own emotional life

This chapter has explored aspects of sharpening up language for feelings and emotions. The next chapter extends this to focus upon two relatively simple, practical and easily memorized maps of our basic innate and learned human emotions, of which there are only some six of each.

5
CHARTING OUR
SIX INNATE EMOTIONS

5
CHARTING OUR SIX INNATE EMOTIONS

'The only hard facts...are the facts of feeling. Emotion and sentiment are incomparably more solid than statistics. When one wanders back in memory through the field of life one has traversed, in diligent search of hard facts, one comes back bearing in one's arms a sheaf of feelings'.
Havelock Ellis, 1859-1939, *Selected Essays*

'We nurse a fiction that people love to cover up their feelings; but I have learned that if the feeling is real, and deep, they love far better to find a way to uncover it'
David Grayson in *The Friendly Road*

Emotion is in the loop of reason all the time. Our experience is always emotionally loaded.
Antonio Damasio, neuroscientist, 2003

A working distinction has been made in chapter 4 between feelings and emotions, the latter being helpfully viewed as more fundamental. It is helpful in moving towards greater emotional mastery to map out our basic emotions, to find something akin to the chemist's periodic table of the elements, yet not so complex, which fits well enough with experience.

This, and the next chapter, outlines a relatively simple scheme that meets our need in this arena, and which is not in any fundamental variance with such scholarship as is available.

5.1 Mapping human emotions

A crucial distinction is made between our *innate* and *learned* emotions; those that are on the one hand present at birth in our common chromosomes and nature, and those that, on the other hand, are the consequence and product of our social learning after birth. In this chapter we address the innate emotions; and in chapter 6 the learned emotions, of which it is argued that love, so crucial to all our living, is one, yet of a somewhat different kind, and so is followed up more fully in chapter 7.

Two complementary diagrams are central to the presentation in this and the next chapter. Diagrams 6 and 7 are complementary halves of a 'map' or 'working model' for humans' emotional structure. The model as a whole is a simple, but not simplistic, outcome of my own long reflections upon relevant evidence, experience and practical application with individuals and groups. It seems to provide an easy-to-remember backcloth, a core framework for improving our emotional management and performance, so getting our heads and hearts more attuned.

5.2 Six universal innate emotions

Studies of human populations in very different anthropological settings have revealed a marked similarity in emotional expressiveness shown through dispositions of the eyes and facial muscles when presented with similar stimuli based upon common stories. Both video and photographic records have been tools in such controlled studies. Facial expressions for basic emotions are similar across the world. Hence aspects of former cultural theories of emotion have been discredited. Yet the biological commonalities within our innate, though not the learned emotions, enable us to face our behavior more from the shared perspective of the human family. Even babies born blind make facial expressions typical of basic emotions through smiles, grimaces and so on.

Diagram 6, in tune with our nature, displays six fundamental innate emotions; 'innate' simply meaning that these are present at birth in all humans, regardless of culture or ethnicity. These emotions are named as:

Joy; sadness; anger, and *fear,* plus *hunger* and *distress.*

The last two of these emotions are named slightly separately because they are also innately physiological, as well as being psychological, responses. The six instinctively innate emotions with their 'potential energies' are shown as segments in the diagram. Other explanatory words, linked or associated with the core emotions, are shown outside the central circle, while the notes and table appended to this diagram give further explanations concerning possible conceptions of each emotion being, or feeling, positive or negative.

Diagram 6: Innate human emotions

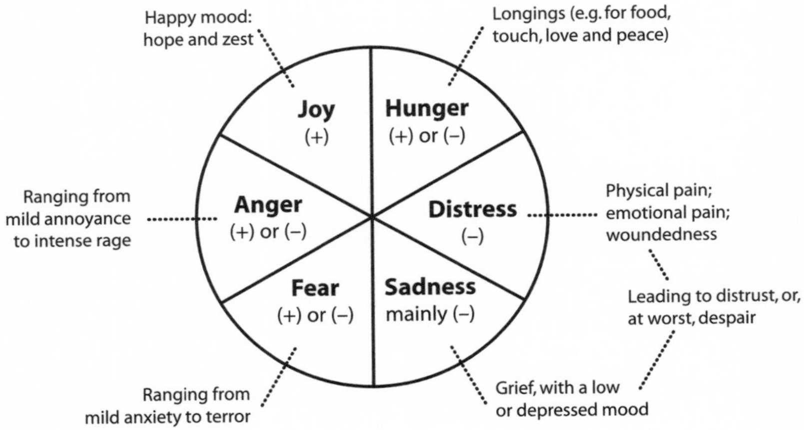

Happy mood: hope and zest

Longings (e.g. for food, touch, love and peace)

Joy (+)

Hunger (+) or (−)

Ranging from mild annoyance to intense rage

Anger (+) or (−)

Distress (−)

Physical pain; emotional pain; woundedness

Fear (+) or (−)

Sadness mainly (−)

Leading to distrust, or, at worst, despair

Ranging from mild anxiety to terror

Grief, with a low or depressed mood

Notes concerning this diagram:
1. The six basic emotions in the circle segments are experienced relatively swiftly through the more primitive limbic brain, and associate with related feelings or 'compound' emotions.

2. Hungers, longings and the pains of distress, are each associated with body physiology, while sadness has an advantage of prompting us to recognize past regrets, and to acknowledge the losses and imperfections that are a part of life.

3. Three of the six innate emotions can move between positive and negative bi-poles of consequence, depending upon personal balance, as summarized in this table.

Innate Emotion	Positive Aspect	Negative Aspects	Positive stimulus for
HUNGER	Gives drive to satisfy valid needs for survival and growth.	Greed (for food, sex, drink, money, power, knowledge); jealousy, exploitative lust.	Health of mind and body. Self-discipline and respect for others.
FEAR	Warns of danger, provides sense of direction and discernment about safety.	Over-anxiety and panic, uncertainty; possibly overly critical attitudes.	Coping and worldly confidence; making decisions.
ANGER	Drive that gets things done; can energize as well as protect.	Malice, destructiveness, violence and loss of control.	Creative energy and shedding tension.

4. The other three innate emotions are clearly positive or largely negative. While some people report that sometimes they grow as persons through pain, hardship, hurt and sadness, only significantly disturbed people actively seek such experience.

5. Some have suggested 'surprise' and 'disgust' as innate emotions. However these seem to have learned aspects and so are noted in the second half of the model (chapter 6).

Everyone can understand this innate six-segment model, and

moreover remember it for application in reflections upon experience and feelings in everyday life. Almost every feeling that we experience can, I suggest, be tracked back at least in part to these six basic, innate emotions. Most of our describable feelings can thus be viewed as secondary 'compounds' of the 'elemental' basic emotions, to adapt again an analogy from basic chemistry. Table 9 illustrates these.

Table 9: Innate emotions and related feelings

Innate Emotion	Related Feelings
Hunger $\oplus$ and $\ominus$	Longings (e.g. for food, sex, care, touch, peace), ravenous, thirsty, famished, lustful
Distress $\ominus$ (both physical and emotional)	Pain, hurting, aching, numb, tiresome, wounded, agonized, tormented, sore
Sadness $\ominus$	Dejected, grief, despair, depression, hopeless, helpless, miserable, unhappy, distrusting
Anger $\oplus$ and $\ominus$	Miffed, resentful, displeased, enraged, furious, hateful, violent, murderous
Fear $\oplus$ and $\ominus$	Anxious, worried, troubled, fretful, nervy, dreading, terrified, panicky, intimidated
Joy $\oplus$	Merry, glad, hopeful, cheerful, enchanted, exalted, delighted, blissful, pleased, radiant

When innate emotions associated with our basic needs (section 2.2) are not sufficiently met, negative consequences are likely. For example, someone who is very hungry for food may be both greedy and disrespectful around a meal table. Someone who feels discouraged because many new experiences 'go over their head', and who is therefore not comprehending, is likely to feel confused, helpless and sad. Someone who lacks love, or is given no arena for responsibility, may be both angry and anxious. Someone who is more hungry for personal power than to use a social or professional position to serve others is likely to be insecure, or deep-down fearful, or even depressed.

Next we examine the six innate emotions in more detail.

5.3 Characteristics of the basic emotions

5.3.1 *Hunger*

This emotion is fundamentally associated with our *longings*, both physical and psychological. Mostly these longings are very primal, that is associated with senses and processes of survival. For example, we have a regular physical need both to feed and to defecate; these are innate physiological hungers. Others include closeness and affirmation through physical touch, in some circumstances expressed or longed for sexually. The basic human needs encountered in section 2.2 also embody our basic longings and hungers.

Interestingly, and challengingly, in our society there is a range of emotionally based, primal eating disorders, including anorexia (a form of self-starvation, that if unresolved is a slow form of suicide), and bulimia (periodic binge eating followed by enforced food dumping). In such conditions normal food hunger becomes disturbed, most frequently amongst image-conscious young women, many of whom seem on the surface to have much going for them in terms of worldly success. The late Princess Diana was a famous example of this kind of extreme suffering, which seems to be associated with low inner self-regard, of which perfectionism can be a distorted part. One recovered anorexic has described her earlier condition as follows:

'My illness started as my career took off. I had worked
my way up the career ladder very quickly. My anorexia
was perhaps a silent way of (my body) saying stop all
this responsibility and expecting so much of me ... for
my perfectionist nature meant I put every last reserve

of energy into my job, but the tank was running on empty.'

Lucy Elkins, *The Times*, 8th August 2000

This quotation raises the central issue of *energy flows* and their conservation in all our lives, both physical and emotional. Our life 'outputs' or consequences in terms of useful work, and inner equanimity, and, externally, being reasonable and responsible with others, quite simply depend upon the 'inputs' we receive. Our 'in-tray' includes, in particular, healthy food and drink, sufficient regular sleep, times of reflective relaxation, the interest, collaboration and friendship of others, emotional and spiritual nurture, and new learning relevant to our practical tasks. The 'storage tanks' of our human 'machinery' need regular topping-up with balanced physical and emotional diets to supply our innate longings. If we ignore these requirements over long periods of time there are prices to pay in terms of lost efficiency, not only for ourselves, but others close by who depend upon us. So it is vital that we understand, recognize and name the variety of our legitimate hungers, and that we monitor them, ensuring that they are met by responsible means.

Anorexics, at their extremes, starve themselves of everything, as if driven by a death wish. Perverse neural circuits arising from inadequate nurture basically trick the body to shut down on food hunger. Then most other aspects of the personality begin to close down also, including feelings, friendships, comfort and even the touch of another person. It is as if a bizarre searching for the next outlined innate emotion, *distress*, becomes the mission of whatever life is left. This is, of course, no less than a slow pathway to suicide.

There is a deep perversity in this type of emotionally disturbed response that applies far beyond the particulars of anorexia. It seems that *any significant earlier primal wound, if unredeemed, retains a capacity to replicate itself later*. Given often very different practical circumstances in which the brain's emotional system is being stretched, perhaps many years later, an old and deeply hidden circuit of wounded-being (rather than well-being) may leap against present environmental circumstances and demands. This is an example of a widespread phenomenon termed 'the cycle of emotional deprivation' that has the propensity to transmit through generations (see further chapter 7).

The prevention and redemption of primal wounds within us is arguably the most important challenge facing humanity. This is a huge issue to which this text can only occasionally allude, but is commented upon further within chapter 11. The clear balance of research, still largely ignored in public policy and too many private choices, shows that ensuring that all the basic innate longings of babies, infants and young children are reliably met is the most cost-effective option.

Cures for the tragic self-neglect amongst anorexics, or the body-abuse of bulimics, involve depth psychotherapy, sometimes aided by drugs, in order to rekindle and heal the wounded inner-spirit. This is not simply a health, but also a spiritual issue, as are all matters of 'the will to live'. Deep healing in most cases of poor mental health involves forming more life-giving productive neural circuitry to which the inner will says 'yes', while actively refusing to listen to the deformed garbage of old inner 'tapes' or 'read-outs', however formed in the first place, that prompt later self-abuse.

5.3.2 *Distress*

Like hunger, distress has both physiological and psychological aspects. We associate the word distress with unpleasant and painful sensations. Distress is in respects the price paid for our being conscious and having the capacity for intense feeling.

Physical sensations pass from all regions of the body through the central nervous system to the brain. Physical pain is carried by two types of nerve: one 'fast' that transports sharp pain, one 'slow' that carries a deeper burning pain. So, for example, when we bump ourselves in relatively minor ways, and then 'rub surface pain better', the surface stimulation blocks off some of the immediate sharp pain.

The neuro-physiology and chemistry of pain and distress is complex, and there are some significant differences between individuals. Tears upon distress are uniquely human, and a relatively accurate signal of pain. Positive thoughts within the sufferer or the focused compassion of another person can reduce the level of pain experienced, so, for example, hospital visiting is frequently far more than merely social. Detail of the links between the physical and emotional arenas of pain need not concern us here, but it is the case that when significant numbers of our cells are damaged, by bruising for example, we feel hurt because we cannot avoid participation in their collective feelings. Here however we are more specifically concerned with emotional pain, triggered by emotional wounding whether in the past or the present.

We live amid the reality of an imperfect emotional world. Nobody has ever been perfectly nurtured and cared for with sensitive consideration at all times by perfect parents, perfect teachers, neighbors, employers and so on. Hence everyone has experienced insensitivity, some emotional imperfection, hurt, damage and disappointment felt consciously or unconsciously as emotional pain. In my opinion, most of that sort of pain is never actively intended by others holding duties of care. Rather it is the product of the emotional and relational blindness that our culture has yet to take seriously.

Sometimes we are treated by others, and also treat others, with some kind of deliberate intention to hurt emotionally and, though probably more rare, also physically. Such behavior always implicitly requires us to reflect and to examine ourselves, in addition to the circumstances, motives and make-up of others. However, some at least of the apparently deliberate wounding which goes on in everyday life, including marital and work conflicts, has some unconscious elements that essentially perpetuate the prior wounds of the emotional 'aggressor'. Those wounds of course may have nothing to do directly with the 'victim', who, understandably, may be tempted to protest and fight back.

Many emotional wounds have their origin in *lack of attention* or inconsiderate attention rather than open hostility, the overall issue at stake being unmet hunger and longings. Attention is crucial, because people hollering in emotional pain, however hidden it may be, find it hard to attend seriously to the needs of others. For them the serious consideration of another person is difficult, as their wounds over-ride their beings. Such people are seriously unable to get inside another person's emotional shoes, or appreciate the practical demands upon them. This contributes towards making them difficult to get on with, or to live with. At worst, unattended souls may become habitually criminal people, whose behavior thereby further drives away the gentle and reliable attention for which, underneath external bravado, they crave.

Whatever the childhood situation, if emotional neglect is inadequately attended to, and to a degree re-nurtured in adult life through the 'therapy' of patient good friendship, spiritual reflection, or more specific 'clinical' therapies, the sad and destructive cycle of emotional wounding referred to above is likely to perpetuate (see further diagrams 10 and 12 below). In a busy world, with life now for too many akin to a frenzy of hurry sickness, there are many dilemmas concerning our giving serious enough attention even to those whom we love very dearly at crucial phases of life change. Deficits in relational focusing have health and spiritual costs. As irrational and over-busy bees, we pay severely for our lack of serious observation and attention to each other.

Amid the perversity of distress, most people live with a sense of hope that there is a less painful world worth working for, and are affirmed in that faith by the presence of at least some shafts of joy in our lives when things are going well, and not least when sad or unpromising situations are turned around. There is thus a redemptive element possible through distress and pain. Although none of us in our right minds seeks distress, it is a part of life that many down the ages have put to good use by staying with difficulties, to tap them for the hidden strengths they may draw out to the point of healing when, as CS Lewis put it, we may be 'surpassed by joy'.

5.3.3 *Sadness and grief*

If a joyous zest is at one end of the spectrum of human feelings, then depression, an extreme form of sadness, is at the other, with melancholy and grief somewhere in-between. If joy is akin to a multicolored rainbow of light, sadness is grey, and depression black.

We can feel sad at quite trivial things, such as a wet day, the end of a holiday, failure of garden seed to germinate, disposing of a pair of shoes that has served us well, and so on. Within some of these sadnesses there may be tinges of anger. Associated with sadness may be grief from a loss, perhaps of expectation, hope, proximity of friendship, fidelity, job or home, or bereavement through death of a close other. *Grief*, as an expression of wounded emotions, is our reaction to disappointment, hurt or loss of what we might reasonably have expected, and is always relational.

Grief demands a reassessment of relevant parts of life, and has both good and ghastly potential (see chapter 11, diagram 12). 'Good grief' has a pattern over time in which there is eventually a 'bottoming out' of sorrow, followed by a new equilibrium becoming established beyond the loss. 'Ghastly grief' on the other hand, which may prompt depression, occurs if the 'hole' of sorrow perpetuates, a new equilibrium being elusive. Movement through the process and phases of grief can be facilitated by some public and private rituals; for example, a memorial service, or reassembling some photographs, or having a heart-to-heart chat with a friend. Such activities extend and warm the emotional mind, while excessive isolation or intrusive forms of socializing seem to impede grief recovery.

Depression is a form of sadness, often without any easily discernable foundation. In this state, life is drained of meaning, and the resulting depression can take many forms. For the depressed person, life is virtually falling apart, seeming an endless collection of pointless events. Its manifestly non-objective essence is a loss of all faith, and of all hope; a crisis of faith in any part of creation, with an apparently total loss of memory of anything that has been good and worthwhile in the past. Such feelings, when all is dark, sad and bad were well known to the Psalmists of the Old Testament, alongside elations of recovery from 'the pit'. The psalms can be a rich treasure for all of us during periods of feeling low.

Depression is becoming better understood, but its neurological electrochemistry, like almost everything else in the brain, is complex. It has been speculated from brain imaging studies that much depression is caused by the *amygdala* firing off negative feelings into the conscious. There, in parts of the cortex, long-term memory circuits that match the low feeling are reactivated. The depressed feelings are reinforced and become locked in, as though nothing more uplifting had ever existed. The thalamus (diagrams 4 and 5, pages 62 and 65) then tends to keep the whole perverse circuitry alive. Antidepressant drugs essentially raise neurotransmitter levels to switch on circuits for better emotional balance, calming those that are perversely overactive. Again, a reservoir of loving nurture and tender loving care from babyhood, is a protective factor, reducing the chances of building perverse brain circuitry.

The incidence of depression in our culture is now high, and a majority of visits by patients to general practitioners have emotional origins. Depressions are commonly triggered by circumstances that shake a person's self-belief and esteem, so that they feel they are effectively losing control of their circumstances, as happens for example in redundancy or long-term unemployment, or in the suddenly unwanted chosen departure of a spouse or partner. Youth suicide, particularly amongst young males, is a serious issue in many economically developed countries, having many contributory factors, including the sense of meaninglessness, yet largely unrelated to material circumstances. Suicide, like most mental health issues, is far more linked to emotional than to material poverty.

Chapter 11 examines aspects of common depressive feelings and their (non-clinical) management in the context of the quest for happiness.

5.3.4 *Anger*

While people tend to view hungers and their implicit longings as mostly legitimate and often harmless, and are compassionate towards sadness and distress, anger tends to be an emotion regarded culturally as rather shameful, perceptions of the emotion being much more associated with the negative aspects noted in the table accompanying diagram 6.

Anger, both our own anger and that of others, is perhaps the most difficult of our basic emotions to manage well. Most anger reflects our need or desire to object or fight when our inner or outer world feels threatened, let down and uncomfortable. This is in contrast to fear, which we will note next is more concerned with escape or 'flight'.

There are two paradoxes concerning much human anger. Firstly, we do not tend to get angry about matters or people that are not important to us, it being pointless to waste the energy of anger on things that we do not care about or are indifferent to. Secondly, some of the intense anger that we may feel is only let out and actually displayed in contexts where, subconsciously at least, we feel safe, and where those on the receiving end are likely to put up with it, or feel they have no choice but so to do. This is the backcloth to at least some domestic situations. One may, for example, feel furious with one's boss at work, but generally circumspect about expressing it as, probably, rational fear wins. Less so with one's parent or spouse, who in addition to whatever angers may be expressed about their personal behavior, tend to listen to those angers bottled up from elsewhere, from school or workplace for example. Some of the options for the handling of anger, an emotion that, if given full rein, gets many into trouble in the social world, are addressed in the next exercise.

While on the one hand anger is often visible, as facial expression, temper and rage, all of which tend to make the world a bleaker place, much may remain properly invisible as we learn of pro-social ways to handle our anger. However, an individual who denies all anger in his or her make-up is not living in a real world, and may in consequence be impaired in a variety of ways, known perhaps only to those very close to by. Blocked off anger is un-assuaged and unhealed anger. Some of this may be resting in the unconscious mind from much earlier in life when there may simply have been no available language or safe circumstances in which to express it.

Our responses to our own and others' anger are in practice very varied. When two people get angry and show the emotion at the same time, one probably triggered by the other, we have a real argument. This, even when excess drink or drugs are not a part of the picture, may escalate to huge proportions, drawing in, in all probability, a whole host of other simmering past hurt material that is not relevant to the particular starting issue of concern. Most married couples know of such tensions, and must, in love, learn to manage them creatively if the relationship is to thrive. One tactic chosen by some spouses may be to be silent while the other 'blows off steam' and subsides. Such incidents involving streams of irritation and frustration are an almost inevitable part of family life. Couples who say that they never have disagreements either repress their feelings very effectively, or have found mutually collusive ways of engagement that deliberately avoid tension.

Children tend to have more angry emotional outbursts than adults; incidents of temper tantrums are commonplace in infants and adolescents. The still developing rational cortex of the immature young brain is often no match for the power of the *amygdala*. Hence the short-route response to a disliked incoming signal, such as a correction or control order from a parent, predominates, while the thinking cortex is mostly by-passed (see diagram 5, page 65). However many adults are also not adept in monitoring and handling anger constructively, taking out their hurt feelings unjustly on others.

The three distinct sections displayed as Table 10 show, first, eight commonly used methods of handling anger, followed by two separate sets of good and ugly coping examples. It is suggested that you reflect on this display carefully. Perhaps you may decide to discuss with a close friend a particular anger issue that you sense at present; possibly your own anger, or someone else's anger towards you or perhaps someone close to you such as your child. Reflecting and talking calmly about anger helps with its safer management. Hence a personal exercise (15) is also provided.

Table 10: Options and examples in the handling of anger

1. Main strategic options (methods people tend to use; only two are commended*)

Charming and repressed on the outside, but furious inside with bottled-up resentment.	Displace and/ or release anger through other activities: e.g. art, writing, clubs, exercise, pets.*	Deny the anger, and quietly block it off by a repressive buttoning-up.	Take the anger and disperse it on the innocent.
Hit out physically.	Shout and threaten.	Stay calm; reflect, meditate or pray.*	Cry openly or alone.

2. Ugly coping examples

Deliberate irritation of others; drive fast and recklessly, slam doors, bully or vandalize.	Run away from home or partner. Seek gratification; be promiscuous; get pregnant without lover's proper agreement.	Take to drink or drugs; or go on excessive spending sprees.	Deliberately exaggerate or lie.
Blame loved ones.	Kick or punch somebody.	Acts of arson, rape or stealing.	Close the ears; attempt suicide.

continued...

3. Good coping examples

Start to monitor the triggers of anger, and their frequency.	Start a reflective journal about feelings; read a relevant book; begin art therapy.	Seek helpful mediation or counseling.	Buy and use a punch bag in the garage for safe energy release.
Persevere over resolution of key conflicts	Calm in communication.	Play for time; move to safety.	Call on a close friend.

Personal exercise 15

This exercise is about your the handling of your own anger, and your reactions to displays of anger of others. You may need to have two quiet reflective sessions to deal with the whole of this exercise. Display table 10 (above) should be of some help as you engage with all of the items 1–6:

1. Give two examples of things that tend to make you very irritated or cross.

2. Is the likely level of your anger to a situation more or less constant, or does your irritability also depend upon other factors?

3. For the two examples you have noted, reflect upon and record your behavior in coping with the possible progression of angry feelings as follows: mild irritation to annoyance, to anger, to temper and rage, to violence.

4. Note how you tend to react when someone gets angry with you. Does there tend to be any difference depending upon whether the angry person is a loved one or someone more distant?

5. Record from experience your views on 'buttoning up', that is, repressing anger, and what you see as good and bad consequences of so doing.

6. Reflect upon whether you might be able to reconfigure aspects of your anger seen perhaps as a kind of friendly advance warning signal for your attention. Record an example where you might try this out, and your hopes in so doing.

5.3.5 *Fear*

The potential for particular fears associated with survival seems to be hard-wired into our brains at an early stage. It is rather like a faint memory trace of things that have proved harmful to our species from way back in the evolutionary past. Fear is essentially associated with the flight from potential or actual danger.

In social terms, especially among males, fear tends to be associated with an inability to cope with the world. Males tend to be socialized into 'macho' frames of reference. Tribal expectations are that, in appropriate contemporary ways, males will become something like the warriors of past eras, showing boldness and physical strength, courage and bravery. These are seen as virtues, though those are far from being simply physical. Even though males have an enormous range of physical and other characteristics, many males still feel a pressure to be fearless, though this sometimes results in foolhardiness and bullying.

Babies show instinctive withdrawal from certain stimuli. There seem to be natural fears about such things as sudden and sharp noises, snakes, big spiders, swooping birds, the harsh growl of a dog, and also of heights. These are protective fears, extended in later learning to other hard-textured moving objects such as cars, to angry or harsh faces, and to a vast range of circumstances perceived as or later taught as threatening to personal safety.

Minor anxieties and debilitating phobias or terror are at opposite ends of the fear scale. Probably most of us have a wide range of more or less free-floating anxieties associated with fears that everyday things may not work out well. We may worry about being late for an appointment, missing a train, losing our wallet, forgetting a pin number, and so on. Most of these anxieties are far from being life threatening, but they are associated with a tidy order that, for the most part, we have invented to help us to feel good and secure. In the case of lateness for an appointment for example, although we may never have had anyone reject our apology, or refuse to see us or get angry in consequence of our lateness, the anxiety can arise mainly because we feel we have violated our view of what it means to be considerate to another person, and so our self-image internally may be more threatened than the fear of rejection.

In our socialization and prior experience we may develop a distorted view of what is genuinely to be feared. Some people at least can learn to be comfortable about snakes through becoming informed about their real dangers. Others overcome the natural human fear of heights through developing competence and confidence in climbing. Many have irrational fears of flying in airplanes; irrational in the statistical sense that there are far more risks in crossing the road and using other forms of transport. There are now special events that aim to counter that kind of fear, associated with what is a real loss of personal control.

Frightening memories from stressful events, such as a road accident, can become etched directly into the limbic system and then the frontal cortical lobes to prompt excessive later fears. Post-traumatic stress counseling seeks both to calm, and in some cases to recover memory of terrifying experiences that have left people in deep shock even if they have not been physically injured. The aim is to return clients to normal functioning lives without unhelpful new fears. But fear also has a constructive function as a friendly warning device. A life without fears might seem at times to be very attractive, but it would certainly be shorter!

5.3.6 *Joy*

This last of the six innate emotions causes us no difficulties, except perhaps our longing for its presence, even to the point of a certain jealousy, close to the learned emotion of *envy* (see chapter 6) when we see it clearly within others. Joy is the outcome of a deep sense of well being, and more available to us than most of us realize, particularly if we take our spiritual nature seriously. This, as we will see later, does not necessarily require us to become outwardly religious. Joy is a sense of living life with a genuine zest, either while alone or in others' company. This emotion is related to both an inner and outer sense of sufficient security, and of pervasive meaning and purpose, and is seen in people of all ages. Tears sometimes accompany this emotion, though these tears have a different chemical composition to those experienced through pain and distress.

Clearly joy is far more than a positive response, through laughing, to humor. Indeed much humor is related to human pathos and misfortune, and even suffering, albeit usually in bizarre situations. Great comedians, Charlie Chaplin and John Cleese for example, both recognize and use their own depressive sides creatively to make others laugh.

Joy too is deeper than a passing feeling of happiness such as we experience when we receive a birthday card, or our favorite sports team wins, or we pass a test. Its three key components are: physical comfort or pleasure, a sense of reliable nurture (a protective factor that keeps potential negative emotions from the *amygdala* at bay), and a sense of cohesiveness and meaning. This last component is influenced by holding a world view of things as working out well overall, something that may be provided by a sincere sense of spirituality.

We may think of joy as an active and deep contentment, more of an inner presence than an outer signal. Joyous people tend to smile much more than they frown, are likely to have a mature sense of humor, are excited and zestful about life, and are simply good company. If we try to package up our joy in some kind of selfish separation from others we find that it slips through our fingers. So joy is fundamentally a social emotion in celebration of shared life, and flowing with love's deep rather than superficial energy. Joy therefore comes partly from confidently surmounting the barriers between people through sharing both our feelings, and activities that enhance our sense of personal significance and meaning.

In chapter 11 we return to aspects of the quest for happiness, encountering what it means to be content, engaging with the many ongoing touches of life that are so necessary for our general health. Having here outlined the six innate emotions, we need to note that they are not experienced in watertight compartments. The innate emotions are interlinked within the limbic system and cortex, and sometimes flow into one another. For example, sadness may turn to anger, and anger is frequently an element in depressive feelings and behavior. Also, distress and joy may intermingle, and hunger may trigger fear, as we have noted.

Personal exercise 16

This exercise provides some revision of the demarcations outlined in this chapter. You are asked to complete the 16 blank cells of a table similar to that shown. An example is provided first in order to help you in this task.

Basic emotional disposition, frequently experienced	A likely consequence or result: act, think or feel	Balance of results: plus, neutral, minus?
1. Food hungry	Many snacks or binge eating	Minus
2. Touch and sex hungry		
3. Longing to see a lost relative		
4. Anxious about traveling		
5. Joy		
6. Pained by disease		
7. Sad and lost in bereavement		
8. Raging		
9. Despairing		

Finally, for one of the exercise examples 2–4, record a possible positive outcome if you have not already done so.

From this account of the innate human emotions, viewed as a kind of universal language that could, at best, bind humanity together as a single family, we now move on in the next chapter to the second part of the model of emotional structure. This is the *learned* emotions, those emotions that we are not born with, but which we may learn through cultural immersion during life, given a fair wind of social experience. As we will see, love is classified as a learned emotion, though it is far more than an emotion, more a gift of commitment and care as is explored on more detail in chapter 7.

6
OUR KEY LEARNED EMOTIONS

6
OUR KEY LEARNED EMOTIONS

'Feelings are conditions that cause us to change,
and to alter our judgments.'
Aristotle, 384-322 BC

'Pure are all the emotions that gather you together and lift you up;
impure is that emotion which seizes only one side of your being
and so distorts you.'
Rainer Rilke, 1875-1926, in *Letters to a Young Poet*

It was noted in chapter 4 that our elemental innate emotions and their associated compound feelings just *are*, in the sense that they exist, and are neither right nor wrong. Hence, in their essence at least, though not necessarily in their practice, they demand no particular ethical judgment. In this chapter we turn to the important and complementary *learned* emotions in order to examine their nature. *Learned* here means that such emotions are not inborn, but the products of our cultural experience and social learning *after* birth.

6.1 Mapping the learned emotions

Diagram 7 lays out the main *learned* emotions as a further pattern of six, that complements diagram 6 of innate emotions featured in the previous chapter (page 98). The emotions are shown in an equivalent pie chart, with associative links beyond the circle, and explanatory notes following.

Diagram 7: EMOTIONS LEARNED IN SOCIAL SETTINGS

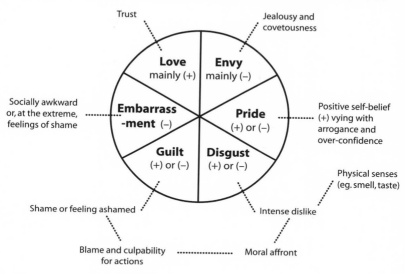

Notes concerning diagram 7:

1. As with the innate emotions, each learned emotion might be perceived as being positive, negative or, according to circumstances, a combination of the two.

2. Due to the many different social and cultural conditions in which people grow up, there seems to be more variation in the ways in which the learned emotions are expressed compared with the innate emotions. Learned emotions are nonetheless an important part of relationships and therefore of social cohesion.

3. Love is helpfully seen as the gift of a *commitment* from another person rather than as simply an emotion. Serious love involves our thinking as well as heartfelt feeling.

4. Learned emotions involve at least some processing by the sophisticated and evolutionary advanced parts of our brains (the *cortex)* that lie above our more primitive basic

emotional centre, that is a cluster of tiny structures (the *limbic system*) that we noted in chapter 3 lie just above the spinal brain stem.

5. Mostly we experience the learned emotions at a relatively slower pace than the innate emotions because the stimulus signals have to travel further along our highly complex brain circuits. We may, for example, have seconds or minutes before we feel embarrassment, but we can lose our temper in anger almost instantaneously (see diagram 5).

6. Surprise, that is, recognizing the unexpected, has been suggested as another specific emotion. Something unexpected implies prior learning of what is common or normal, like sunrise, a parent returning home, or cars being driven on the appropriate side of the highway: when we are taken by surprise we are startled, our senses are stimulated. We are stopped in our tracks by such a stimulus that demands our attention and readiness for response. I prefer not to include this feature as an emotion here, though it is clearly related to our being attuned to threats and fear, and so has some innate qualities of sensation.

Beyond note 3 above, little more will be said in this chapter about *love* felt as an emotion, but involving much more, particularly a personal commitment, making love essentially a *free gift* from one person to another. Much cultural confusion reigns regarding the topic of love, which is far from being a one-dimensional quality, existing in different forms, as we will see in chapter 7.

6.2 Particular personal emotions: envy, pride, disgust and embarrassment

In this section we examine four of the six learned emotions shown in diagram 7. Envy and pride are listed amongst the so-called seven deadly sins that are enshrined in some cultural traditions (see further exercise 18 following). The positives and negatives shown alongside each learned emotion in diagram 7 might suggest that envy, and the associated jealousy and covetousness, are largely 'deadly' emotions, rarely helpful to those sensing them, tending to convey that a person's life 'drinking glass' is less than full, whereas, more likely, it could be sufficiently full.

Jealousy is common over matters of intimate love, the pull of possessiveness vying with that of permissiveness. It can be argued that such particular love, if genuine, is bound to merit protection, with jealousy being an aspect of the way that such care and protection is likely to function and become expressed; to be otherwise would perhaps signal an indifference that is far from love's call. On the other hand however, mature love is not claustrophobic; it extends trust and allows the other sufficient space to grow. Hence intense jealousy, with its strong, controlling and over-possessive powers, rarely aids relational resolution; at worst it prompts scheming, coercion, and even violence.

Material *envy* and covetousness are emotions played upon every day in promotional advertising of many kinds. Acts of real moral courage are now demanded to question peers and loved ones who are perhaps becoming too addicted to shopping and to the very latest fashions, items of which they already have plenty and which still have much useful life in them, such as a car, mobile phone, computer, a dress or pair of trousers. On the other hand, if the envy is of some human performance (rather than skin-deep bodily appearance), that is, envy of some skill, or even of another person's integrity and spirituality, this may help to raise our realistic sights and aspirations, and can be viewed as positive. Likewise, an intense envy, desire and thus passion for fairness and social justice at a civic and democratic level may reasonably be seen as a virtue.

Pride, says an old adage, 'comes before a fall'. This refers to an arrogant, over-confident and unattractive puffed-up pride, rather than justified self-belief through 'proper pride' in a job well done or a courageous stand of principle taken. So pride can work both for and against us. More often than not, puffed-up pride, and the frequently associated displays of bragging, reflects some basic personal insecurity. This kind of pride is used in an attempt to bolster a person's confidence. Of course, deep down in the quiet of their inner being, people who use this know that it rarely works. However, taking a modest pride in ones' own children, and for them to sense this, is arguably a parental duty of encouragement, unless, as in some cases, it shifts to subtle forms of parental bragging in order to bask in their children's reflected glory.

Disgust is an emotion of intense dislike, and seems to have some innate, instinctive aspects. Our eyes, and senses of taste and smell, are each seemingly programmed to flee from certain sights, flavors and odors that may harm us, such as faeces and rotting foodstuffs that harbor parasites and infectious bacteria. The learned aspects of disgust are associated with disapproval of others' behavior (for example poor table manners or picking one's nose in public) that reflect, according to upbringing, particular conventions rather than fundamentally moral issues. However, most of our learned disgust arises from a sense of ethical affront to our deeply held values, our moral sentiments. Examples are cheating at sports or board games; blatant lack of consideration for others through deliberate deceit; sexual exploitation; foul language or drunkenness, and all forms of false witness, and so on. Our disgust is likely to become heightened if these behaviors do not seem to be accompanied by any sense of personal responsibility, shame or guilt on the part of the offender when bad behavior is reasonably pointed out (see the linkages shown near the foot of diagram 7, and also section 6.3 following).

Embarrassment is an emotion associated with degrees of awkwardness that we can feel in particular social situations. This is a sensing that we do not fit and are misplaced in context. This can happen when we feel out of tune with the majority present at an event, whether in terms of appearance, dress, accent, manners or ethics, or, alternatively, when we are perhaps offended by some matter of language or omission on the part of a loved one who is accompanying us on a social occasion. Examples in the first category might be not having all the correct kit when turning out for a sports team, dropping food at a formal dinner, when acting as a party host forgetting someone's name, or telling a joke when nobody laughs. Examples of the second category could be ones' spouse scorning the partner of one's boss or otherwise being indiscreet, perhaps under the influence of too much wine, or when a toddler reveals to a visitor a burn mark on the carpet that has been covered up discretely by a rug.

It is a part of human make-up to wish to feel fully accepted within at least some groups, no less than our desire to be accepted by particular people. This need, requiring some conformity to group expectations and habits – the local 'rules' - trivial though they may seem such as etiquette at golf and card games, sometimes vies with our desire to be different from the crowd. Indeed human feelings within group contexts are an important arena (see later sections 10.4 and 10.6). Nor is social embarrassment simply a feature of mature adults, for it is commonplace for adolescents to be, on occasion, embarrassed by their parents' demeanor and behavior as they seek to establish some separate sense of identity amongst their peers. Within a few years, our children may turn the tables from being the focus of parental embarrassment!

Personal exercise 17

Record brief notes, including any particular reflections, concerning one personal example of each of the following:

- A persistent personal material envy or jealousy.
- What you regard as improper parental pride.
- Behavior, your own or someone else's, that fills you with disgust.
- A memorable embarrassment.

6.3 Our moral emotions: guilt, shame and blame

Guilt, as one of the six learned emotions, is associated closely with shame, or feeling ashamed, as noted in diagram 7. *Shame*, felt as what we can call a 'moral' emotion, arises from living and learning in a social group, or groups. All groups (including gangs and criminal groups) have their own implicit or explicit *moral codes* of acceptable and unacceptable behavior. Common moral precepts include 'you shall not steal or tell lies', and 'you shall consider others before acting'. When such code precepts are breached, a sense of social shame is likely to be experienced. This is the result of both teaching, largely through the barely conscious actions, or engrained 'tribal habits' of elders, and the resulting and mostly helpful group pressures shaping social attachment as more than mere conformity.

Feeling ashamed is in its turn closely related to feeling guilt, while shame for some socially disapproved action is linked with blame, that is, culpability and accountability for the action. Blame is not itself a feeling or emotion, but being blamed and also found guilty is also to be shamed. These words collectively are termed 'moral' emotions because they are associated with views of right and wrong, and judgments of human action, both our own and that of other people, within a social and cultural setting. The terms as such do not contain particular moral values, though the intellect is also involved in learning and practicing moral principles and linking them with or superimposing them upon our feelings and emotions.

But morality itself is not innate. *None of us is born moral, only with moral potential.* We learn to become moral, or otherwise, mostly through the ways in which we are treated as children, supplemented by more formal initiations into frameworks of moral rules and precepts as we grow older. Moral behavior, like love as we shall see further in the next chapter, mostly grows from being given the gift of consideration. In other words, we learn to behave ethically principally by being treated ethically rather than by edict. Learning intellectually about ethics is likely to have little impact upon behavior unless the ethics in question are explained by others acting as esteemed role models, exhibiting and drip-feeding considerate behavior during the everyday.

Guilt and shame are closely connected, while blaming is not strictly a matter of feeling or an emotion, but is much more to do with perceived responsibility for undesirable happenings. Dictionary definitions make this clear:

> *guilt*: a feeling that one is to blame for some undesirable happening, possibly including a legal offence;
> *shame*: a feeling of distress or humiliation, disgrace or discredit caused by consciousness of one's guilt or folly having done something that is wrong or regrettable;
> *blame*: to place responsibility for or to attribute misfortunes, being happenings with bad results, to a person or group of people.

Thus shame and guilt are what people feel inside when they believe, or our encouraged to believe by others, that they have done or thought something regrettable or wrong. In some respects, these feelings involve psychological punishment for behavior disapproved by a kind of 'parental voice' that lies within us all, and is an aspect of practical conscience. Letting this guilt go and placing or projecting responsibility elsewhere may involve blame.

Blame is the human activity of attributing responsibility for bad happenings onto specific other people, or of sometimes accepting the responsibility ourselves. This sort of judgment, or placing of responsibility, may trigger or enhance guilt and shame in others, or in ourselves. Either way, whether the attribution of blame is just or otherwise, there are burdens to shift (in the case of 'projecting' or scapegoating blame), or to carry (in the case of accepting blame), some of which may only be relieved by a combination of apology and forgiveness. (Note that *projection* of emotions, both an important psychological concept and a very common behavior trait in both private and public life, is encountered in more detail in chapters 9 and 10).

Personal exercise 18

By way of summary, humans share two types or classes of important emotions: the six innate at birth, and about the same number acquired through learning as we grow up with others in social settings. These are brought together is this display.

Innate	Fear	Joy	Sadness	Anger	Distress	Hunger
Learned	Love	Envy	Guilt	Pride	Embarrassment	Disgust

Most of the learned emotions have associations with what we, or society, regard as 'right' or 'wrong', and so include a moral aspect or tone.

Tradition has it that there are 'seven deadly sins': pride, gluttony, envy lust, covetousness, sloth and anger. 'Sin' however implies wrong thoughts or actions or both.

Record your reflections about these 'deadly sins' in relation to the summary display of emotions. In what ways do you believe that the 'deadly sins' tradition is misplaced and astray in the light of the emotions shown in the tabular display?

Personal exercise 19

Distinctions between shame, blame and guilt having been outlined, make notes of five separate personal examples of:

(a) when you tend to feel ashamed

(b) when you properly blamed yourself for something

(c) when you properly blamed someone else (or a group) for something

(d) when you *im*properly attributed blame elsewhere, and

(e) something you are still feeling guilty about.

Note any fresh personal actions that you think are still called for concerning (d) or (e).

A sense of *guilt*, which like so much else in the arena of emotions, has its origins in our childhood, has both positive and negative aspects, as shown on diagram 7, page 119:

Positive: brings us into touch with our accountability for our personal conduct and of the need to consider others while respecting ourselves, and is a prompt for making appropriate apology and reparation.

Negative: can make us feel unworthy, incompetent and unlovable, or, at worst, some kind of unforgivable 'mistake of creation'.

When we consider our overall mental health in relation to our wrongdoings, mistakes and misjudgments, we have to find a balance between the positive and negative aspects of our sense of shame and guilt. After all, those feelings arise from what may sometimes be the courageous acceptance of personal accountability, especially now that we tend to live in a culture of blame and litigation. Herein lies the challenge of searching for emotional balance, and that demands of us essentially three things:

1. To acknowledge the imperfections within our selves, and in the wider world without having self-esteem or hope radically undermined. We can make mistakes and still remain basically fine people, particularly if we have done all we reasonably can to make corrections or reparations where possible.

2. To recognize that the concept of social justice requires a price to be paid for culpability, whether by way of a sincere apology, specific reparation, or formal punishment for being guilty of causing others' misfortune.

3. To take hold of the healing power of forgiveness. If this is not given directly by others while there is serious remorse (an inner problem for those 'hard of heart'), then self-forgiveness, or indeed divine forgiveness can still be grasped. We are not meant to harbor our own guilt beyond due time.

Personal exercise 20

This exercise concerns the personal mistakes or misjudgments that we all make from time to time. These are situations in which, later on, we wish we had acted differently, all with the benefit of that tantalizing quality – hindsight. These may be errors, or 'sins' of omission or of commission by intent. Our mistakes and misjudgments generally have their prime origin in some feature of ourselves, for example through impatience, 'trying to cut corners', or to 'penny-pinch', or through tiredness, stress and forgetfulness.

For each of the seven listed 'origins of mistakes' (or as many as you can) make a note of a personal example and give it a 'guilt-rating' on a three-point scale:

0 (zero guilt), 1 (low guilt), 2 (high guilt).

Origins of mistakes:

- Had insufficient or incorrect information at the time
- Misdirected energy or over-enthusiasm
- Not telling the truth to myself or others
- Joined a crowd against my better judgment
- Over-indulgence or greed
- Procrastination and delay in doing something necessary, and
- Not paying due attention with ears or eyes.

You might now care to add up your overall 'guilt score', and note how you feel about that in relation to the score range of zero to 14.

For everyone, living is a matter of making the best of both what we shape and what crosses our paths, and of coping with, and working on, our fallibilities and imperfections. Those having a perfectionist kind of disposition, however that was acquired, often feel guilty for not living up to their own unrealistic high standards, and that may prove problematic for others also. At the other end of the spectrum are those who tend to deny that things are not well, and believe that they are culpable for nothing.

Some people who have been taught through harsh and over-corrective parenting early in life, or later discouraging teaching, too easily see themselves in a poor light as under-achievers, and generally unacceptable as they are, and so develop too little inner confidence or self-esteem. Often of a timid disposition, such people in some family or peer groups become easy scapegoats, even sometimes to the point of feeling responsible for ensuring the happiness of all other members of a group. In a way such sad people become their own experts in guilt, self-blame and deprecation, with the unsurprising consequences of feelings of wretchedness, quiet desperation, and probably eventually depression interpreted as their 'just dessert'.

All of us need from time to time to inspect our opinions of ourselves, and see that, however we arrived at them, these are not immutable truths. We are in fact quite free to change them, for there are many costs to ourselves and those around us, if we carry excessive arrogance or guilt as the foundation of our world.

6.4 A mid-point summary

Having explored our emotional, rational and relational natures, and some of the language that link the three; then having examined aspects of brain function and mapped both our innate and our learned emotions, and hopefully engaged you in at least a few of the personal exercises, a brief summary is appropriate at this mid point of this text.

Human beings across our globe have the same kinds of bodies, and the same kinds of brains and minds. We share the same evolutionary history, though until very recently, separated for the most part by unknown geography and limitations in mass travel. Within that divergent history we have developed a wide range of cultural variations concerning how our bodies are used and our minds have adapted to environmental circumstances. Our differences are skin and culture deep. We and our ancestors became smarter compared with the rest of the animal kingdom because we are able, given the fair wind of cultural encouragement, to use our unique capability of reflection on our practical and social situation, and to combine our emotions with our huge capacity for reasoning.

Yet we have reached a point where materially advanced societies, partly through democratic ideals, rely less on holistic wisdom, of which materialism is only a part, so placing our sustainability and continued evolution at risk. This book takes the stance that harm can be minimized and health maximized if populations become seriously literate in the arts of reflection and of minding and mastering emotions. We need a fair wind of cultural encouragement to assist us in becoming more emotionally intelligent. This suggests that we must learn to make distinctions concerning when to control our emotions, and when to be controlled by them. Taking revenge when hurt, for example, may have some imprint in us biologically, but it is rarely wise, and usually leads to escalations of damaging action. At whatever level, the arts of diplomacy, of mediation and apology are emotionally and practically to be encouraged.

We have seen that our universally shared chromosome systems (see also section 9.1) with their gene variations, hard wire and etch our six innate emotions into our neural circuitry, and that these are not fundamentally influenced by culture. On the other hand, the socially learned emotions are greatly influenced by cultural circumstances for their particular expression, reflecting the human brain's great plasticity in responding to social environments. However, being a fundamentally social species, our innate and learned emotions inevitably interact within each of us as living organisms, so that boundaries between the two classes of emotion are in practice blurred and shape more of a spectrum of emotionality.

Noted also is that our values intertwine, and arouse emotional responses. Thus our emotions can stretch our aspirations and imagination beyond that which pure reason would allow. Such recognition helps to correct the flawed balance of intellectual view in post-renaissance western societies that our emotions have a net impediment upon intelligent behavior. The reality seems to be that intelligent beings that lacked emotions could barely evolve. So we face the reality of a spectrum of human emotions that no legislation can take away. Moreover, there can be no lasting and secure escape into pure intellect; neither into one of a blinkered scientific or economic determinism, nor to one of moral, spiritual or religious fundamentalisms, however appealing they may be to our longings for short cuts to personal security.

Our emotions are within the scope of the loop of reason all the time. So, wisely, we must work with our emotions to ensure that reflective reason also gets into the loop, not least when we are in tight corners of opportunity for growth or destructiveness, to maximize their potentials to enrich rather than damage our lives. There is no ethically neutral haven of pure logic or computerized robotics where we can escape their influences. Human character is far beyond the reach of simplistic naiveties of material logic and economics. Perhaps most crucially, our emotions, when seriously reflected upon, signal a range of our most worthy priorities; areas reflecting the significance and essence of our lives.

At best, over the whole range of our human performance, nature combines with social nurture to achieve optimum maintenance, creativity and equanimity. Within that, love, a topic replete with emotional undertow to which we turn in the next chapter, is our best and most advanced social purpose, combining emotion with good reason, and so providing the finest glue for optimum social collaboration, sensitivity and peace.

7
LOVE IS AN INTELLIGENT GIFT

7
LOVE IS AN INTELLIGENT GIFT

'We must begin to love in order that we may not fall ill, and must fall ill if, in consequence of frustration, we cannot love.'
Sigmund Freud, 1856-1939

'Where love rules, there is no will to power; and where power predominates, there love is lacking. The one is the shadow of the other.'
Carl Jung, 1875-1961, in *Psychological Reflections*

'Figuring out how to love people is the hardest thing of all - because we finally get so careful, having been disillusioned one way or another. You lose confidence - and love after all is an act of confidence.'
Arthur Miller, *Timebends: A Life*, 1987

'To be capable of giving and receiving mature love is as sound a criterion as we have for the fulfilled personality.'
Rollo May in *Man's Search for Himself*

It has been well written that 'love makes the world go round'; also that 'there are three things worth having in life: faith, hope and love; yet the greatest of these is love'. Love was assigned in chapter 6 as a socially learned emotion. This tends to surprise some people, yet being 'born to love' (if that is our fundamental purpose) is a very different statement from being 'born *with* love'.

Yet love in its many ramifications, and enacted in many diverse contexts, is not simply emotional. This was alluded to in chapter 6. As with guilt, it is only partly appropriate to view love in emotional terms, since deliberate *acts of will* by individual minds are involved. So humans assent, with at least parts of their conscious will, to *give* a commitment to love another person. If this is reciprocated in mutuality, the two parties also agree to *accept* the love being offered. Of course this can involve many deep feelings, and such commitments, implicit or explicit, are advisedly not entered into lightly.

But our first port of call concerning love focuses upon what we are to understand of love's nature in its varied forms.

7.1 Forms of love

Most of us believe that love in its varied forms is a distinctive human quality. But it is not inborn, hard-wired into our brains; yet we have an imprinted longing to be given this precious commodity in forms that feel reliable. So love is recognizable when it is given sensitivity, and it is a *potential* embedded in our natural need. The four quotations above embody truths for reflection in this crucial life-enhancing or life-denying arena.

At the heart of so many of the personal and social problems that we experience in our seemingly freewheeling society are difficulties about receiving, giving, feeling, experiencing and knowing of 'reliable love'. Yet, as noted in section 2.2, our need to experience reliable love is no less basic than our need for fresh air and clean water. Many psychiatric disorders seem to be associated with feeling unloved, and the often associated avoidance of commitment and risk of suffering that a truly loving 'for better for worse' relationship entails.

Popular songs frequently use the 'love' word, yet most often in sentimentalized contexts. A famous song track of the Beatles' simply announced that 'All you need is love; love is all you need'. Many such statements embody truth, rather than merely superficial romanticism. What they generally lack is insight into love's nature as well as guidance about how it might be propagated. So long as popular culture emphasizes 'falling and feeling in love', or animalistic sex drives, there is a strong risk that only those time-limited 'drugs' that help us feel exotically high are being suggested as our need, when our nature is much deeper.

Love's nature is of several basic kinds, each having associated emotions, in particular:

- *filio:* brotherly or sisterly friendship and companionship;
- *eros:* sexual affections, passions, desires; not necessarily 'making' other loves;
- *storge:* a warm benevolence, affection or liking; and
- *agape:* an unselfish and unconditional caring for another person's whole being, in which the lover's own need for love is essentially secondary.

Here the ancient Greco-Latin roots are shown. The *agape* form of love is the deepest variant and strongly associated with Christian tradition. Its gift is associated with a commitment and promise, what for many in previous eras was called a covenant, and also with the presence of compassion. It implies a willingness to extend oneself in order to give nurture to another person, and to encourage their rounded growth in relation to appropriate phases of the life cycle. Such love is intentional, involving choice and ongoing action, including keeping the person in heart and mind when not physically present with them. Thus *agape* love is far less fickle than the ups and downs of any passing feeling, emotion or desire, and requires a sufficient degree of self-love and respect for its reliable delivery. There can however be no love without friendship, and beyond animalistic desire and fleshly lust, even *eros* love presupposes friendship. Such sentiments are summarized in this poetic fragment:

> *Love says,*
> *With neither thrusting need, nor rights:*
> *'Here is friendship, mindful insights;*
> *A listening voice, touch in tenderness;*

For you, in the now,
And the ever,
Of your blessedness'.
Adapted from *Transformations,* page 31

Since we all need friendship, and compassionate and companionate love to be sustained in our individuality, the fullness of love requires mutuality, both of giving and receiving.

This *triangle of love-forms* helps to make some further important distinctions.

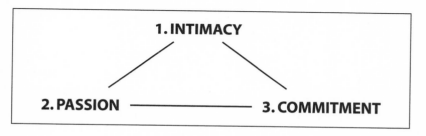

On this model:

- *Consummate* love would be described as 1 + 2 + 3
- *Romantic* love would be akin to 1 + 2 – 3
- An infatuation, or *eros* love would be 2 – 1 – 3
- *Compassionate* love or soul friendship would be 1 – 2 + 3
- *Dutiful* love would be 3 – 1 – 2
- *Indifference*, which is non-love, would be none of 1 to 3.

Of course no relationship is ever static, and so the kind of consummate love that most of those who marry dream of, is most unlikely to be felt as ever-present. Love over most of a lifetime is sustained sometimes by dutiful love, and for most couples the passion and intimacy certainly vary. The commitment is fundamental, sustained despite circumstances.

Personal exercise 21

This exercise requires you to review the relative closeness, or felt intimacy, of important people in your life. In respects this extends Exercise 2 in chapter 2.

Place your first name in capitals in a small rectangular box at the centre of a fresh side of paper (perhaps A4 size turned round 90 degrees from 'portrait' to 'landscape'). Jot down separately the names of the people (both family and others) who are important in your life, perhaps up to about twelve names. Now place, one at a time, these names on the main sheet at distances from your name according to how close you feel presently to each person. Arrange the names around the centre box so that you can draw in connecting 'spokes' from each of the other people to your own name. When you have finished your diagram, write notes about your feelings about the result. Make a note of anything that you think and hope might be realistically changed through your own actions in the relative closeness of any particular people. You might consider talking in confidence with the person closest to you on the chart about this exercise.

7.2 Falling and feeling romantically in love

We can better understand the nature of 'true' love (that is the *agape* form), and perceive how this fits around the fabric of our emotional lives, if we first clear away some of the undergrowth concerning romantic love, or simply 'feeling in love'. Anthropologists have recorded common indicators of the phenomenon of romantic love in some 90per cent of disparate cultures, so here seems to exist a universal phenomenon. Each culture has its own variations of expression and expectation of romantic love. In the West, though love 'at first sight' is rare, the element of surprise is common, as are the distorting ideas that romance is a fine foundation for a long-term commitment and the supreme form of self-fulfillment.

'Falling in love' is usually a temporary phase in which boundaries of the ego-self melt and a person's totality, even their soul, becomes centered upon and preoccupied with the beloved. Usually the beloved is another earthly person, but a few also use the phrase in relation to works of art and music, or of their love of God. For this to happen, some vacancy exists in the lover's life that the person of over-riding fascination is felt to fill. The desired one tends to be endowed with perfection by a dream-like projection from the lover onto the beloved that, in all likelihood, will in due course be impossible to live up to. In respects this phase of loving, which may turn out to be an immature infatuation, is a period of deep irrationality; a craziness to be savored, and of course to be enjoyed for what it is, but not of itself a secure foundation for important long-term life decisions or of a mature faith.

Whether spoken or not the feelings of the lover are frequently of the kind 'I need you, and I need just as much for you to need me', 'I want you for ever', 'I cannot live without you, and can think of nothing else'. Such real and genuine feelings are a wrenching combination of dependence, ecstasy and pain, an affliction of lovesickness that separation, however brief, finds very hard to tolerate, as if the lover is on the edge of a terrible grief and pining. In this state, rationality is brushed aside, as the totality of reality is overtaken by feelings entirely focused and projected upon the beloved.

There is of course a real 'chemistry' involved when this happens between two people. Euphoric feelings are enhanced by the secretion of several substances into the bloodstream, especially phenyl-ethylamine, triggered by signals from the brain. These give that 'head over heels in love' sense, a special but inevitably diminishing 'kick'. For an enduring love, when emotionality and rationality become synchronized through reflection and acts of will, a different set of chemicals called *endomorphins* seem to be triggered to take over. If this kind of love is not reciprocated, there may be, at worst, wasted years of useless suffering; unrequited love is indeed a harsh form of punishment.

In summary, the following can be safely said about 'falling in love':

a) There may be no conscious choice when falling in love, for it is an erotically linked and temporary emotional experience, revealing a vacant need. When it happens, the choice element is restricted to how we tackle, handle the move through the experience.

b) If the feelings are not really reciprocated, the lover is basically infatuated, yet also deeply in need of real love.

c) In respects the process is one of psychological disturbance, unhealthy and not self or other enlarging since it promotes an over dependence of self upon another; and that is an immature and over-needy form of love.

d) It can be dangerous and lead to deep pain and misfortune unless followed by the parties seeing, through disclosure, each other's imperfections amid their separate identities and life stories.

The deeper love that is craved comes not through the moving 'meltdown' of mutual feelings, whatever forms that takes, but through many shared activities beyond this phase. It is these that cement commitments and create reliable bonds, slowly forming the chemistry and faith of trust. Within trust, ideally, there is no acting out, but simply a mutual psychological and physical openness, and paradoxically along with that an inevitable vulnerability of the kind reflected in Gillian Rose's words quoted in chapter 1:

'There is no democracy in any love relationship, only mercy. Each party, woman, man, the child in each relationship is absolute power as well as absolute vulnerability.'

Table 11 summarizes the main contrasts between romantic and friendship love.

Table 11: Romantic love's contrasts with mature friendship love

ROMANTIC LOVE [Passionate-projective love]	FRIENDSHIP LOVE [Permanent, potent 'promise' love]
Based upon feelings and the projection of perfection. Infatuations imaged by e.g. Hollywood and romantic novels.	Committed to the other within a pattern of sustaining, healing and growth. Aware of other's deficiencies and weaknesses.
Boundaries of a personal self have dissolved; attachment is obsessive within what is in respects a mental disturbance.	Partners sustain a sense of their separate personal selves, each enriched by the attachment.
Eros-sexual elements prominent, even obsessive and rampant.	Sense of constancy and underlying security, with respect for quiet.
Buzz of romance the key yardstick to assess relational quality.	Ready to serve the other within the everyday. Enjoy small tasks.
Sense that personal happiness is external and within the regular gift of the partner.	Personal happiness is seen as an inner achievement; demands on partner realistic.
Intense feelings tend to oscillate wildly; need big events to bolster good feelings.	Content in the moment, with the other as he or she is; appreciate the ordinary.
Sense of the spiritual locked solely into the other person in relationship.	Personal spirituality quarried within the self, drawing on the unconscious and the shadow.
Ready to criticize if the 'divine' image held of the partner tarnishes, as it must; demands on partner can be unreasonable.	Affirm and encourage the other, rather than judge according to a misplaced 'divine' image; demands reasonable and realistic.
Personal shadow not owned, only sensed and experienced beyond the self by projection onto others.	Good level of self-knowledge including owning downsides of own shadow; regular practice of personal reflection.
Great dependency upon the partner, with a repressed, unexamined unconscious.	Both partners well formed as individuals; sharing without excessive dependency.

7.3 Individualism, choice and commitment

Over recent decades there have been cultural shifts towards an ethos of individualism, now often reflected in public policies. Personal autonomy, individual adults' rights and tokens of social equality have gained supremacy as cultural ideals, thus shifting our presumptions about personal behavior. Pressured by economics and materialism, mostly unshackled from the ethics of mutuality, attitudes reflecting 'me' and 'my', have tended to gain ascendancy in discourse over those of 'we' and 'our'. Imperceptibly personal behavior has tended to shift away from obligation, commitment and trust, towards personal choice, self-fulfillment and personal pleasures. Yet those 'goods' are generally dependent upon others' collaboration or company. Quite simply, other individuals and social units (of family, local community, workplace and region), are almost always vital for personal fulfillment.

Tenuous relationship commitment begets inner insecurity. This applies not only to children but also to adults in, for example, employment and commercial transactions, in the operation of the law, and in matters of faith. A world without promises, mutual trust and social reliability would grind to a halt; even stock markets could not function!

The term 'relational holocaust' was referred to in section 1.3. Many have or are being deeply hurt from not having their commitment in intimate relationships reciprocated in the inevitable ups and downs of life. While superficial judgments of personal circumstances are unhelpful, deserting partners or parents are not culturally encouraged to work for love's deep patience, and often leave behind human wreckage, more wary of bonding, and deeply unsure about becoming psychologically attached again. The cultural result is a widespread loss of inner confidence about mutual trust and reliable loving, mirrored in this solo mother's words:

> *'I wanted to marry him, but he wasn't keen. Good job I*
> *didn't, for though he sees us now and then, on your own*

*you don't have to wonder about anyone else being reliable
or making an effort for you, so in some ways that is easier.'*

Consequences of dashed hopes of partnering and parenting, repeated millions of times over, are more than sad, for they have a tendency to become transmitted down the generations. Tax and welfare subsidies are no real substitute for an absent mate and collaborating co-parent. Intimate relationships have become too easily disposable, often akin to 'sex without strings, and relationships without rings'. Our laws facilitate the process, and education systems barely challenge common heresies concerning love's character. Moreover, there are far too few winners from traumas of relationship breakdown.

Commitment to love inevitably requires constraints on individual choice. Yet a paradox of making a choice is that other choices are forfeited. Nonetheless, the preservation of freedom depends in part upon curbing choice and exercising responsibility so as to sustain some choices for others. Commitment involves being particular, and in human relationships it involves implicit or explicit promising, great patience and a willingness to forgive.

7.4 Love as gift

Learning *about* love in relation to our human nature gives us, I believe, a better grip on learning *how to* love. If we classify love as an emotion at all, it is a *learned* emotion with consequential activities. The activity of loving is a matter of both the genuine delivery of love, and the reasonably accurate perception, and reception, of love. So an active love has to be understood in its essentials, and be both given and received. But the giving of love comes first; and if that is to become sufficiently reliable and distinct from passing feelings, the gift must arise from sufficient *conscious reflection*.

For true love, in this *agape* sense, the commitment includes a willingness to extend the self for the sake of the other even when their current state or behavior is unattractive, disappointing or even offensive. This gift love is not centrally a matter of feeling, nor is it a matter of dependency. It involves kindness, patience, forgiveness and much else that does not evaporate even when personal feelings are neither romantic nor even particularly warm whether through tiredness, or everyday wear and tear. Secure loving involves holding on through good times and bad, and of being reasonably available during times of a loved one's distress. Such love cannot be upon a basis of limited liability, for that eventually limits our ability to love at all.

Gift-love has its own brain chemistry, through the soothing impact of endomorphins, nature's gentling painkillers. We all need that kind of gift, and from birth onwards. Yet the perplexing reality is that we can only give this precious commodity if we have received it in sufficiency. However, given a sufficiency of love, we can all multiply our output of loving, for love is like a 'chain letter' of giving and receiving. Unless we are reasonably securely connected both to others and to our own essence, we are vulnerable to loss of hope and meaning.

Complementing items (a) to (d) for 'head over heels' romantic love in section 7.2 above, we can summarize 'gift love' as follows:

a) It involves the emotions but is more fundamentally an act or many acts of will, commitment, and sincerely intentional rather than perfect promising.

b) It requires proper recognition of individuality and separateness (for two persons can never be just one), and attends to the other's feelings, with careful listening, unselfish attitudes, and allocates 'quality time' for good communication.

c) It requires practical demonstration through shared activities, a judicious giving and withholding, compromise, teamwork, forbearance and forgiveness.

d) It requires faith, or 'risks in trust', and even the paradoxical certainty at some stages of grief and loss.

7.5 Marital love

Marital love is important in all societies, not least because it is associated, though not exclusively, with the welfare of children. Changes in family structure do not negate the innate hope of every child to have good and mutually enriching bonds with their mothers and fathers or equivalent substitutes for them.

In marriage there is a mutual need to be seen, at depth, as *the* most important 'other', with the balance of a partner's behavior appropriate to such status. Companionship, in which each spouse feels respected, understood and loved, is now fortunately seen as crucial. Couples sustaining mutual companionship, along with a dash of the erotic and the dutiful, do not seriously consider divorce.

There is perhaps nothing more important than for a couple to prepare well for marriage and equivalent cohabitations. This is a natural extension of learning of and learning to love. It is all too easy to set sail on partnership ventures in ignorance of the essential dynamics. False expectations can later create tensions and oppositional flows of energy. For example, in the marital 'bed' are six people historically and psychologically, as *three* couples:

1. *He* as her lover, alongside *she* as his lover.
2. *He* as her father figure, alongside *she* as his little girl.
3. *She* as his mother figure, alongside *he* as her little boy.

So each partner inevitably acts in three roles. The experience of marital love includes parental forms of love that aid the healing of at least some childhood wounds, for nobody has been perfectly nurtured. *The ongoing task of the marriage bond is a mutual process of sustaining, healing and growth.* Eros, the sexual element within a mature and stable adult friendship, acts in part as a lubricant in the processes of sustaining in the day-by-day healing from past and present knocks and disappointments, and the continued growth of the character and nature of each partner. No married person quite lives with exactly the same person whom they married; *change is a part of the deal.* Each couple are effectively driving a sort of dual control car, in which each person acts as a 'chartered driver', a 'learner driver' and a 'driving instructor', with, early on at least, the possibility that in-laws are psychologically in the back seats!

If this broad dynamic is understood, it can help prevent the escalation of tensions whose hidden, subconscious, origins often lie in prior biography rather than in the marriage itself. Loving in practice, tested perhaps most of all in marriage, involves securing natural flows of energy that hide within deep longings for connection and for intimacy. In every marital conflict are embedded longings to take apparently disparate dynamic energies down a common path. When people fight it is often from false premises, with threatening and threatened emotions. So hell may be let loose, making forgiveness more difficult.

Neurologically, changing established adult 'mind-sets' is, we now know, far from easy. New ways of thinking and envisioning require new neural circuits to be formed within brain systems. That is impeded if emotions are in active turbulence or defensiveness. Emotional blockages impede our thinking, changes in our outlook and the consideration of fresh ideas, a common enough experience. However, calm reflection allows the thinking cortex its potential to influence and work on changing old mind-sets that are no longer helpful to life and love.

Central in the maintenance of any close relationship, and particularly marriage, are essentially four factors:

- Individual *perceptions, images and understandings of the other*, of human development and life-course *change* (what we may call 'mind frames or maps').
- *Trust* and an understood *framework f commitment.*
- Regular and effective *communication* (active listening as well as speaking).
- Clarity concerning *individual expectations* (worked through in dialogue).

Diagram 8, flowing downwards through time from infancy, gives a pictorial summary of some key research findings concerning marital quality and stability. In interpreting this diagram it is important to note the five broad factors (lowest arrowheads) that directly impinge upon marital quality and stability when populations of couples are researched, rather than specific cases that may show wide variation.

Diagram 8: A path model towards marital satisfaction

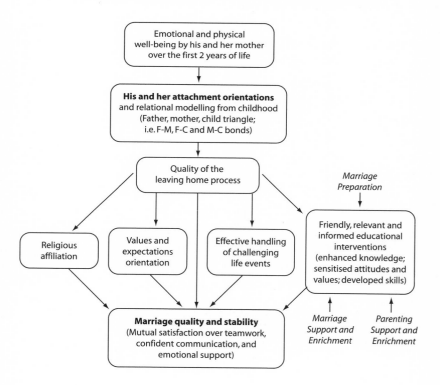

This kind of time-flow path diagram is not one of simple cause and effect, but of significant influences affirmed by the balance of research, and having serious implications for social policy. Studies that sample family members' development over phases of the life cycle are becoming increasingly important. It is clear from diagram 8 that warm parental love and its equivalents are crucial for human welfare throughout life.

7.6   Nurture, affirmation, self-love and will

Searching for and feeling secure within reliable loving from others, as well as appropriately feeding our need for self-love, self-confidence and self-respect, is often not straightforward. Appropriate love and consideration of oneself (a 'proper selfishness') is often no easier within our inner quiet than to love our neighbor, particularly if secure nurture has been in short supply in childhood. Gift love operates like a cascade of nurture and security, as reflected in 'cycles of affirmation' depicted in diagram 9.

Diagram 9:   **Cycle of emotional affirmation**

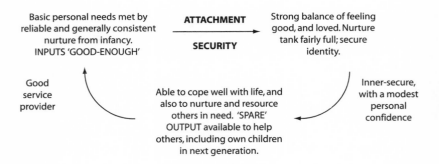

In the cycle of affirmation, with the need of secure love reasonably fulfilled (for no human love is perfect), personal confidence in the inner self grows, and there develops a good flow of positive psychic energy. Little by little this enables the loved one to give attention to others' needs, to give of themselves, and in due course to make commitments as bearers of nurture. In short, the gift of person-to-person love helps in matters of individual will and decisiveness, enabling us to walk through life with a proper confidence. That is grown more from first-hand experience, optimally from infancy, of the patient, generous attention of at least one committed soul-friend, than from academic knowledge and technical skills.

The two fundamentals of cycles of affirmation are:

- An individual's need of love, in principle without condition, must be recognized and sensitively responded to by at least one other, with steadfast predictability, over a long enough period to establish trust.

- The resulting sense of inner security and worth, endows the nurtured loved one with a proper confidence of inner nature and being, so enabling genuine care and concern to be given to others in need. This care and concern may thus grow, akin to a chain letter of nurturance.

'Reliable love' with its corollaries, commitment and promising, involve, as we have noted, conscious and continuous acts of the *will*. The propensity to exercise and sustain the will, as well as give both self and other love, is influenced by early childhood, so the sooner that cycles of affirmation begin, indeed from birth, the better. Over the childhood period a delicate balance needs to be struck between warm social control (which establishes secure boundaries) and some repression of the child's exploratory behavior, especially that which suggests danger. However, excessive coercion of a child's will risks making him or her powerless in terms of later personal control and exercising the basic need of personal responsibility (noted in section 2.2). Everyone needs the confidence of willpower so as to sustain a sense of individual identity and to practice good citizenship.

Personal exercise 22

Do you feel a sense of not being loved or respected when someone close to you is angry with you? If so, make notes about relevant surrounding circumstances. Now reflect on the statement that 'the opposite of love is not fear or anger, nor even hate, but indifference', making notes and perhaps giving illustrations.

What are the main practical ways in which you show your love for a particular person close to you? Note one way through which you might improve your demonstration of this love. Is there one undisclosed way in which you would like your closest love to demonstrate that love to you?

7.7 Love unfelt or unknown: cycles of emotional deprivation

The perpetuating chain of nurture discussed above contrasts starkly with the sad consequences of the alternative 'cycle of deprivation' depicted in diagram 10.

Diagram 10: Cycle of emotional deprivation

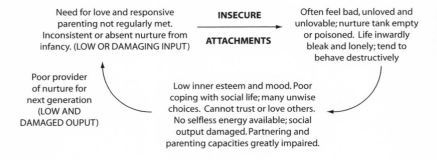

Readers are encouraged to reflect upon the two contrasting cycles carefully, noting how one thing tends to lead to another. Few of us, inhabiting an imperfect world involving imperfect nurture, have avoided experiencing on occasion *both* these cycles, but in widely varying proportions. For each individual, it is the balance of good versus harmful or neglectful input that determines the balance of our behavior and the resilience of our coping with inevitable emotional and practical difficulties as they arise in life.

The negative and positive chains of inter-relatedness, shown in diagrams 9 and 10, respectively reflect the fact that *both security and insecurity, and the trust or distrust that go along with them, become socially embedded and acquire a cultural history.* In these matters the family environment is usually the first and ongoing crucible of influence, aided or otherwise by whatever is available within the surrounding local community to support the dynamics of safe family development over the various phases of life.

Both positive and negative cycles can be broken. Essentially positive situations may be rocked, or more, by unsought catastrophe if events such as bankruptcy, serious accident, debilitating illness, displaced time and energy for relationship maintenance, or a crisis of infidelity (always including unresolved emotional issues for one or more of the parties) are not worked through with patient skill. Negative cycles can also be modified, sometimes strikingly, again by patient, sensitive and deeply caring social and educational intervention.

7.8 The primacy of attachment

Section 2.4 introduced the concept of human attachment, social bonds that grow from attention, care and affection. The child's security of attachment to at least one parent figure by the age of three is probably the best predictive indicator we have for all the key indices of outcome of 'the good life', including educational success, sound citizenship, stability in crucial adult relationships, health prospects, avoidance of criminality, and even IQ and economic success.

For contemporary western societies, studies suggest that little more than one half of children (about 55 per cent) *feel* securely bonded to a parent figure. This is *not* to say that 45 per cent of parents do not love their children. Far from it! But, over matters of human bonds, it is our inner *feelings* about security that count far more than even the very genuine sentiments of others. To know of love in theory is far from experiencing it in practice.

I remember, only too well, an incident when the oldest of our four children was about twelve years old. It was occasionally my voluntary professional practice to give workshops on the growth and development of parenting skills, and associated with that various matters of family policies. Often these events took place on Saturdays, the day when target audiences were most likely to be available. At that time I had a busy Monday to Friday job with many responsibilities and some overseas travel, and was, in retrospect, too often an absent father, my wife being the willing lynch pin at home. One summertime Saturday, at breakfast, I ventured to explain how my day was to be, doing my bit for other peoples' family lives, including those 'less fortunate than our own', when my eldest son said 'But Dad, I wanted you to play cricket with me today, and I have only one Dad to be with.' Of course I loved him dearly, as I still do, but on that, and probably too many other occasions, he and his younger siblings did not feel that love, and my public-spirited justification for my absence probably felt to him like humbug. Love, 'charity' does indeed begin and gets tested most at home!

The balance of all the research on child development was pithily phrased for me around 1980 by one of the world's then most eminent scholars in the field, Harvard's Urie Bronfenbrenner. In a seminar that I attended in Australia (father absence again!) he said:

'The child will thrive if someone, somewhere, is crazy about that kid.'

By 'crazy' Professor Bronfenbrenner meant 'unconditionally committed' to the child's best interests through sensitive nurturing, being both prepared to and able to hang onto the child when rational evidence concerning the child's 'failures', 'nuisance' and antisocial behavior might more naturally prompt a carer's rejection. Sometimes there is a perversity in human behavior in that we may subconsciously behave badly in order to test the limits of the 'through thick and thin' trustworthiness of our nearest and dearest. At any stage beyond infancy, and often in adolescence, youngsters often behave as if to test their lovability. Obviously it is at times such as these that parental resilience is most tested.

The positive and negative cycles of emotional transmission outlined above, are now well informed by many attachment studies. In the absence of interventions, such as new opportunities for learning, there is for example an approximately 80per cent chance of inter-generational transmission of early mothering styles. This means that as parents we tend to copy styles of care or neglect from those who reared us. In respects, this is modern proof of the old biblical saying, amended here, that 'both the sins and the good works of fathers and mothers tend to visit upon kin to the fourth generation'. The need for safe and secure attachments, involving emotional intimacy, is the human relations equivalent of Newton's Laws of Motion in physics. Dimensions of attachment, and the availability of reliable love, constitute governing 'laws of human motion and emotion' ignored by individuals and societies only at their peril.

Poor attachment histories of many well-heeled (though not well healed) celebrities have precipitated tragedy in their private lives. The marriage of Prince Charles to his deceased former wife Diana was a classic high-profile example, a national tragedy no less, that echoed, and echoes still emotionally in millions of ordinary lives. Without sufficient resolution of attachment difficulties, the repetition of negative intergenerational chains remains a risk.

Neither money nor status, nor good looks can purchase secure attachment and its associated heart-brain capacities. The security and strength of any marriage depends to a great extent upon the prior inner emotional security of the two individuals involved. Where one or other party is inner insecure before a courtship, the relationship will need to work on that psychologically as a part of the task of healing, amid the sustaining and growth. Where neither party holds, for whatever reasons, a good-enough reservoir of psychological security, as in the Charles and Diana case, then the marriage will likely experience very real difficulties without early, skilled, therapeutic help. Many marital or cohabiting breakdowns lie in hidden, unconscious wounds brought to the relationship rather than fundamentally generated from within it. Each partner may well be hoping, often unrealistically, for a quality of intimate nurture through marriage that they may never have experienced earlier, and may themselves yet be unable to give without some strategy for personal growth.

Sadly this fact is neither widely known, nor generally understood, yet it can illuminate many an intimate tension. If words can be found to say something like:

> 'These painful feelings, including anger, that I have with you now, and in some ways prompted by what you said and did, are not mostly your fault. Their roots are elsewhere; in my history, even today's history at work. So can you please get alongside me and help me to work through them? Because I love you I hope to do the same kind of thing for you, even though I fail in that sometimes.' ...

.... then a row, or stony silence, over a tension can be avoided.

It is not pleasant for anyone to be held entirely responsible for another person's bad feelings. *Becoming emotionally mature means taking responsibility for the ownership of our personal feelings, whatever the context.* To hold others entirely responsible is to use the phenomenon of projection, encountered later in sections 9.2 and 10.5. Those with experience of community regeneration and of relationships renewal know of the patience often needed by parties for psychological healing, for it is generally very much slower than physical healing.

7.9 Parental tasks and qualities

It is important to recognize that the processes of attachment are not bio-genetically driven, but a social and environmental matter. Early adopted children for example thrive well, and on some indicators even a little better than natural children in two-parent family settings. Good parenting is fundamentally about focusing care through the steady, regular and sensitive commitment of attention. Rearing children, and not least tiny ones, is both intellectually and practically challenging, for never again will their brains, and all their neural circuitry, be growing at such a vast pace. Our family attachment systems need constant renewal, not least through the teenage years when peer group pressures become enormous, calling for different forms of supervision, care and control compared with the early years.

There is no more important civic activity than parents' caring work through home and community life in the rearing of their children. This has huge economic and social benefits that now require greatly increased civic recognition and status. Our children as citizens are our collective future. However, it is not only parents who aid the nurture and maturation of children; all adults have some responsibility, for *it takes an active and supportive community to raise a child.*

Table 12 summarizes important personal qualities in parenting children. These also tend to apply to the 'parenting' of partners and grandchildren. Also shown are the varieties of associated support needed to underpin and to help to optimize the delivery of good parenting.

Table 12: Qualities of and supports for good parenting

Good parenting qualities	Supports required for effective parenting
A balance of outgoing warmth, and of generous practical care.	Secure and safe housing, with a good range of community services.
Committed, actively involved and reasonably well organized domestically.	Sufficient finance, well managed, and balanced with enough time for parenting.
Perceptive and attentive listening.	If possible, the secure love of a co-parent.
Making realistic demands of child's behavior according to its stage of development.	Emotional support and shared tasks and activities with a few reliable friends.
Firm approach to child's boundaries, but not resolutely inflexible.	Opportunities for sharing parenting experiences.
Accepting the role of parent as aiding self-image, and with a balance of joy.	Memories of and good role models of parenting in the present.

Personal exercise 23

This exercise is concerned with a retrospective 'scoring' of the meeting of your key basic personal needs in childhood. From the reasonable balance of your memories, up to the age of about 16, for each of the 10 items listed in the guide table give a rating for each on the scale from 0 to 4 as follows:

0. (not met)

1. (less than adequately met)

2. (adequately met);

3. (more than adequately met),

4. (fully met).

Need of childhood	Rating (0 –4)	Feelings associated
Physical care		
Encouragement given		
Stimulation provided		
A dependable schedule		
Promises made and kept		
Personal space respected		
Affection demonstrated		
Someone who listened		
Helpful boundaries given		
A sense of secure love		
Total (out of 40)		

Now add up your ratings. The minimum score is zero, and the maximum 40. Note your feelings about your total score, along with anything particularly significant within your ratings for each of the ten items listed, using the guide table. If you have known some depression, whether or not you have ever visited your doctor or taken counseling about it, reflect upon whether any of its origins may be related to aspects of your ratings. Again, you might find it both interesting and helpful to discuss this exercise with your spouse, partner or a close friend.

7.10 Love's sanity

In this chapter *agape* love, the kind that is confidently generous in its outreach, and largely without conditions, has been portrayed as the supreme human 'learned emotion'. Involved are many acts of individual will for its fulfillment. Reinforcing the four quotations at the start of this chapter, psychologist Erich Fromm in an important book (*The Art of Loving*, 1957), noted that *love is the only sane and satisfactory answer to the problem of human existence.* Mature love is more a matter of precept than formula (see contrasts in Table 13). It is a learned art and craft, responsive to circumstance, the particulars of time and place.

Table 13: Loves superficial or deep

Fickle loving	Mature loving
Me first, self-centered and taking. Conditional: love *only if* conditions are met.	You first, unselfish and giving. Person, not status or achievement centered.
Changeable and superficial. Resentful and arrogant. Deceptive and manipulative.	Constant, steadfast and deep. Forgiving and patient. Open and respectful.

Much more can be said philosophically and theologically about love and its impacts that move beyond the detail of our emotional lives. Poetry can be a fertile medium for love's nuances. In the poem on the next page I have attempted the impossible, to summarize love's nature.

Obedience to Love

Obedience to love
Is to feel the love,
And yet to will the love
Beyond the volatility
And fragility of feelings.

Obedience to love
Is to be the love
While willing love
Beyond the being.

Obedience to love
Is to scope the love
And yet to hope the love
Beyond mood or mindscape.

Obedience to love
Is to touch the love
With deep tenderness
Of body, mind and soul.

Obedience to love
Is to sleep and to dream the love,
And yet to will the love
Beyond the bedchamber.

Obedience to love
Is to kiss the love
With the gentle confidence
Of love being kissed.

Obedience to love
Is to give the love
Willingly,
Without counting the cost.

Obedience to love
Is to pray for love's providence
As companion and comforter.

Obedience to love
Is to breathe the love
Into thought and action
Beyond each breath,
Even into death.

(From *Lifelines,* pages 60-61, 2004)

Next we turn to some important issues of gender differences in emotional life that tend, too often through ignorance or exaggeration, to harm relationships between the sexes.

8
GENDER DIFFERENCES: HIS AND HER EMOTIONS IN PERSPECTIVE

8
GENDER DIFFERENCES: HIS AND HER EMOTIONS IN PERSPECTIVE

'Different though the sexes are, they intermix. In every human being a vacillation from one sex to the other takes place, and often it is only the clothes that keep the male or female likeness.'
Virginia Woolf, 1882-1941, in *Orlando*

'It is a two-edged sword ... The knowledge that the personalities of the two sexes are socially produced is congenial to every programme that looks forward towards a planned order of society'.
Margaret Mead, 1901-78, in *Sex and Temperament in Three Primitive Societies*

'To fully appreciate being a woman one has to be a man; and to fully appreciate being a man one has to be a woman.'
D.W.Winnicott, 1896-1971

'Don't try to please an overwhelmed woman; just listen to her.'
John Gray, 1996

We live in times in which longstanding cultural presumptions of gender differences have begun to disintegrate, and this far-reaching social phenomenon inevitably becomes experienced in a range of personal readjustments and problems within our home, community and working lives. This short chapter examines gender differences in so far as they are relevant to emotional behavior and capability.

There are some important broad tendencies of gender difference in emotional outlook, having both anatomical and cultural origins, for maleness and femaleness are more of a spectrum of traits than of uniformly sharp distinctions. Nonetheless it is often unhelpful to try to apply these to individual cases and situations. Gender differences need to be kept in perspective, and there are no winners from any falsely polarized 'gender war' that has found various and often shrill expression over recent decades.

8.1 Biochemical and brain and differences

While human males and females obviously have specific physical differences, we are of the same species and only differ in broad genetic make-up to the extent of one chromosome out of forty-six. Only one pair of the 23 pairs of chromosomes that incorporate our gene clusters determines gender, males having one 'Y' rather than a second 'X' chromosome thus:

- Male chromosomes comprise 22 pairs, plus one X and one Y.
- Female chromosomes have the same 22 pairs plus two X.

This relatively small but consequential chromosome difference is present from conception, though specifically male characteristics do not start to develop until about two months after conception, being triggered by the action of the then available male hormone. Initial development is therefore essentially female, and at the very beginnings of life everyone is absolutely dependent on a woman. Chromosomal similarities, and the closeness in chemical structure of the various sex hormones, confer on each of us both a masculine and a feminine aspect. The balance of masculine and feminine traits varies between individuals through both genetics and hormonal levels, as well as according to social and emotional circumstance. Psychologically, we all have some male and female tendencies.

At least some gender differences in emotional interest, intensity and response are related to biochemical factors, particularly the differentiated actions of the main sex hormones. Amongst ovulating females, changes of mood and of thresholds of irritability have been long known, with variations often related to the monthly menstrual cycle.

Aside from obvious issues of reproductive function, some structural and operational differences have been observed between men's and women's brains. The relevant findings of neuroscience so far seem to show that in general the female brain seems to be more *interlinked* amongst its parts. A summary of the differences now follows, with the third and last listed area having particular significance for practical and emotional management.

1. A small and specific part of the right and left hypothalamus (part of the limbic system, see diagram 4, page 62), that is associated with male hormones affecting sexual behavior, is on average 2.5 times larger in men than in women.

2. During ageing, men tend to lose more brain tissue than women, particularly in the frontal and temporal lobes associated with thinking and feeling (see diagram 3, page 60). Such losses may lead to irritability and other personality changes. Women on the other hand tend as they age to lose tissue in the hippocampus (memory connector) and parietal area of the cortex, making them more likely to have difficulty in remembering things and in finding their way about visually and spatially.

3. The corpus callosum, the band of nerve-rich tissues through which the two main lobes of the cortex communicate (see diagram 3, page 60), tends to be larger in women than in men. So too is another much tinier primitive connection between the hemispheres near the limbic system that links only their unconscious areas. In

addition, the connective tissue between the two sides of the thalamus, the brain's 'telephone exchange' within the limbic system (see diagram 4, page 62) tends to be more abundant for women. The physical differences could explain why a greater proportion of women than men seem naturally to be aware of their own and other people's emotions.

Consequent from the differences in this third listed arena, it seems that, in general, women's emotionally more sensitive right hemisphere is able to pass information more efficiently to the analytical and language-talented left hemisphere. In this way women's emotions may be more easily incorporated into their speech and thought patterns than tends to be the case for men, whose emotions translate more directly into action before thought.

Neural imaging studies have shown that men and women tend to use their brains differently as well. When doing complex mental tasks, women tend to bring both sides of their brains to the problem, while men often use only that side most clearly suited to the task. Such patterns of activity can be interpreted by suggesting that women take a broader view of life when making decisions, men being rather more focused, or even having sometimes a 'tunnel vision'. Complementary to this is the fact that the eye function of males tends to have a narrower peripheral vision than that for women. This means that women see out of the corners of their eyes more readily, a useful 'wide angle' trait for tending the broad environment of their offspring, though less good for focusing upon a hunting 'kill' more naturally delegated to males over our long hunter-gatherer ancestry.

Women's sense of smell and of hearing may also be more sensitive than that of many men. Girls' brains in general mature more swiftly than those of boys, except in areas associated with mechanical and spatial reasoning.

8.2 Communicating woman meets action man

Common experience seems to confirm the theory that a woman's two cortical lobes tend to operate as a harmonious well-connected pair, while those of men are more dominated by a pattern of 'one side at a time'.

When a woman has an emotional issue, positive or negative, her first urge is to talk about it, to find words for it and to *share* those words and feelings together with one or more people. It is more likely that she will find another female to take an interest in that emotion and its nuances of language. If she tells even a caring man about her feelings, particularly if they are painful ones, his likely response may either be to make no comment, or to try and 'fix' her feelings. He is likely to see the feelings as a problem to be solved; she experiences them as a reality. He may arrange for some diversionary treat to show his concern, and to take her 'out of herself', or worse, try and soothe her by telling her that her feelings are unjustified and simply irrational. At that stage such male moves can be counterproductive. She does not want her feelings 'fixed', even by her emotionally closest male. Neither does she wish to escape from these emotions. Rather she just wants to be listened to.

Her physiology tends to be more responsive to many nuances of marital interaction that may escape male notice. She remembers both arguments and positive exchanges more vividly than he does. She simply wants her feelings acknowledged and accepted 'in herself' just as she is. For her that acceptance is the very condition for her being able to think things through that she finds imperative before any particular action is contemplated. Thus the dominant female pattern pleads first for communication that will at the same time help her to think and to reason. Seeking to please an overwhelmed woman usually turns out to be impossible; wise guys will simply focus on her and listen to her!

The male response to emotional disturbance tends to by-pass the language centre, and to utilize instead the action centre for problem solving, even when the 'problem' is one of elation, when many men can do almost as many silly things as when they are feeling low, as for example after a tense football match. Men seem to be prompted first to express their feelings through action, whether by flight (using denial as the problem solution), or fight (involving direct countermeasures to fix feelings such as anxiety or anger). Invariably this reaction is unconscious, yet the deeply embedded male 'strategy' leaves the feelings to be sorted out later, or too often, never, for many males perceive that they can survive well enough by emotional escape and repression. Much male cultural formation has long tended to encourage them to do so.

Aside from the biochemical and anatomical differences that have been referred to, my own hunch, affirmed by at least some of the relevant literature, is that men often struggle with dilemmas originating in their early relations with their mothers. Men do not wish to feel victims, and often feel great loyalty to their mothers, who generally did so much that was vital for them while they were so obviously dependent. But there was always that social pressure to grow up and 'become a man', which implies culturally suppressing one's feelings.

Girls on the other hand, at least until fairly recently, become women more naturally, without extra pressure to 'prove themselves', and their femaleness has a stronger line through the reality of maternity. Now, however, female images are in at least partial change, the hidden and overt text being that girls and women 'can do' almost all activities hitherto the preserve of males, from being high-flying executives to football players or presidents.

Much of this widening of gender roles is healthy provided that one crucial social condition, easier said than done, is safeguarded. This is that mothering, and the social nurturing and gentleness of spirit implicit within it, must not simultaneously become downgraded as women feel under pressure to adopt a more assertive, individualistic and even aggressive approach to life. There are ugly aspects of 'girl power', such as the emergence of intimidating girls' gangs, modeled at least a little upon the male counterpart.

Many mothers have felt, and still feel a pressure to encourage their boys to be relatively independent of emotional ties too soon, with some at least being influenced by the partial myth that too much emotional closeness between them and their boys could prompt later homosexual tendencies. Boys naturally feel some ambivalence with respect to their mothers from about the age of two. If mother does not cope well with his swings of mood, need and emotion, the chances of that increase. If she is depressed and under-nurtured for her role, he will tend to perceive her, and, later, other females as either good or bad with little in-between. More ideally the developing boy should find girls and women lovably interesting, and certainly not emotionally threatening.

Now there seems little doubt that, in general, boys are and have been emotionally more vulnerable than girls. However, in early child-care there is still little or no acknowledgement of this. Hence, few mothers are conscious of their likely need to compensate, providing even extra gentling for their boys as a buffer to the harsh realities of male social tendencies. Now many men hide deep fears of male redundancy, given that less muscle strength is required within modern economies and women are adopting many previously male roles, and this requires more recognition if the modern male psyche is to be understood. Aggressive feminism now scares men no less than aggressive masculinity has long scared women.

The later grown-male desire to assuage a woman's emotional pain, often by well-intentioned but unsuitable intervention, may be in part a reflection of male subconscious anxiety, or even inner panic, about feminine emotionality. Some of this may have roots in boyhood anxiety about maternal emotional states; the tug between emotional dependence that dare not be disclosed amid social expectations of 'becoming a man'. Moreover fathers were not expected, at least until very recently, to provide emotional nurture for their boys as an integral aspect of their activities with them. We cannot shift these ingrained patterns without a great deal more insight, forbearance, educational support and wide cultural encouragement. *The emotional gentling of boys and men is thus a huge cultural task.* Simultaneously, and paradoxically, *this is also a necessary aspect of real female emancipation.*

The divergent gender processes and needs within emotionality are summarized in table 14 below, though these are set amid a great deal shared in common.

Table 14: Gender tendencies in emotional response and need

Female response tendency	Male response tendency
Articulate feelings and talk first.	Act first to solve/reduce feeling problem.
Feeling, talking and thinking tend to be simultaneous.	Sequence order: feel, act; later maybe think, then possibly decide to talk.
Accept and sort out feelings first. Communication as a part of the process.	Move to fix feelings first; sort out later. Communication as a tool for delayed use.
Female needs and growth	**Male emotional growth**
Need someone alongside, offering help and support with the felt reality, rather than prescribing solutions.	Need to learn about achieving more on the emotional front by 'doing' less; accepting feelings for what they are.
Need to recognize male insecurity concerning emotional performance, and of its possible antecedents in boyhood.	Must recognize tendency to avoid emotional problems, and face possibility of emotional under-nourishment from parenting norms.

8.3 Opening up emotional stories

If men and women are to improve their mutual understanding amid the changed status and role demands of modern societies, they will need to go with the grain of the gender brain, rather than suppress or fight hormonal, genetic and anatomical differences. Within this task the greater challenge probably rests with men. Men can be aided towards enhanced emotional performance by female encouragement. However, they can also be driven further into their shells, or into trite sarcasm and combat, by aspects of female aggression that have characterized some aspects of women's emancipation.

For many years I have felt that *society needs many more gentle women to encourage the 'coming out' of gentle men.* Of course that is sometimes an impossibly tall order for women who have been badly hurt or exploited by some of their emotionally illiterate and self-centered menfolk. There is nonetheless a 'double bind' here. The generally hidden, unintended emotional and soul wounds that boys and men have been presumed to be impervious to, are in fact often deep-seated triggers for male defensiveness, insensitivity, arrogance, anger, and even violence and criminality.

The emotional development of boys lags behind that of girls from at least as early as the primary school, aided and abetted by a wide range of traditional 'macho' cultural influences that are perceived to demand the repression of the potential emotional repertoire of boys. In general, as most secondary school teachers well know, boys tend to mature in a whole range of ways rather more slowly than girls through puberty and adolescence, and this contributes to communication difficulties between the sexes, not least about emotional life.

Of course for the majority, at some stage beyond puberty, encounters with the opposite sex include discovery and negotiation about physical intimacy in which a wide repertoire of feelings and emotions is inevitably involved. Here it is not appropriate to go into details of these kinds of encounter, which may well happen more than once in a lifetime, and with more than one person at a time. However, underpinning every reasonably serious relationship of this kind, and going beyond the more superficial issues of sexual libido, are matters of fundamental emotional formation and growth. We noted in section 7.5 the reality that when man meets woman in intimacy, present also are a boy hoping to find in the woman aspects of good mother-nurture; and a girl hoping to find in the man aspects of her ideal father-protector. 'Head-over-heels in love' couples need to be aware of the likely inner visitations of projection of ideal figures upon each other that need maturing if the relationship is to thrive.

Couples experiencing erotic love are only generally aware of their roles as male and female lovers, and so fail to appreciate the wealth of latent emotion that is an unavoidable inheritance from their childhoods. No adult is all the time in adult, 'grown-up' mode. *In respects, the child we were, is forever with us.* That once-developing youngster provides barely conscious echoes, not least in emotional tight corners that we inevitably encounter within family life, as well as sometimes in the context of stressors in employment.

Hence well-founded relations of friendship and in marriage or cohabitation will be concerned to explore each partner's prior practical and emotional story that unavoidably influences their attitude and performance in relating. Such sharing, aids the growth of both the love and respect that each longs for, and requires active and open communication practiced until that becomes habitual, as if on autopilot. There must be an atmosphere of calm and of empathy in which each party is sufficiently affirmed; and one of speaking non-defensively and of listening intently, qualities that most men have to work hard to model.

Personal exercise 24

This exercise is concerned with the articulation of your feelings about a chosen adult member of the opposite sex, someone with whom you need to have a good relationship, though not necessarily involving any sexual intimacy. Hence possibilities may be a brother, sister, or work colleague aside from partner. Use your notebook as follows:

    1 Name the person and describe your own present emotions about him/her.

2 Record what you believe makes this relationship worth developing.

3 Outline what you feel to be this person's basic emotional disposition.

4 Has the relationship already overcome some difficulties, and if so, how?

5 Is there an area of conflict sensed with this person that really needs working through? If so, what is this, and how might it be best approached?

(Consider what are you likely to have to guard against in order to secure a path through the conflict; for example, avoid harsh criticism, contempt and defensiveness of your own attitude, seeking both to bridge and to heal.)

Now, select a suitable time and place to explain non-confrontationally to the person you have named in this exercise what you have been reading and reflecting upon, as a basis for a hopefully calm and honest discussion of the issues. Allow the other person some time to consider the same elements 1–5 that you have covered in your notes. Finally, record your views concerning the development of the relationship, and outline your current associated feelings.

8.4 The imperative of gender collaboration

Levels of comfort in the emotional relations between the sexes, like so much else in our relational lives, are set within the overarching phases of human development, in which male and female share very similar needs over the life-course (section 2.2) Table 15 summarizes some important general gender traits, and complements the contrasts given in table 14.

Table 15: Some supplementary emotional comparisons by gender

Females	Males
Motivated by feeling cherished.	Motivated by feeling needed.
Want to be devotedly cared for.	Want to be trusted and admired.
Need reassurance and respect.	Need appreciation and encouragement.
She requires validation as she is.	He wishes to be approved of as he is.
She longs for understanding.	He longs for acceptance.

This chapter has endeavored to avoid unhelpful or even false polarizations concerning gender differences. Men and women are basically complementary, while for many of life's essentials they are fundamentally made for collaboration with, and the mutual support of one another. Within their shared encounters lie three basic psychological tasks: to sustain one another in the everyday present, to give mutual encouragement for personal growth and appropriate change, and to be sources of healing and comfort for whatever past and present wounds. This remains the case whether or not couples conceive children, though childrearing tasks do make major extra demands upon couple relationships. The joys experienced in having children inevitably bring fresh challenges as young people, in their turn, grow unevenly towards maturity.

In the evolutionary pattern, males and females are made for mutuality and appropriate collaboration. The most fundamental element of this is the procreation of and the safe rearing of the next generation. If we are to be appropriately rational, those *procreative and nurturing tasks*, that *set the scene for all emotional agenda and response, require status, recognition, resources and support* in all cultural settings. Such basics within life patterning can never be taken for granted. In the contemporary context, both men and women still hope to pair for long-term emotional and practical support. The educational and cultural implications of this are immense if the huge costs of relational misperception and mismanagement, that prompt serious instabilities and what is often great emotional pain, are to be seriously addressed.

Fortunately we seem to be moving beyond at least some of the harsher aspects of the gender wars of recent decades. The male psyche has been badly dented, as much through technological change as through the growth of assertive feminism. Many opinion-shaping women have moved from a phase of being freedom fighters, and now admit that they are rather more 'struggling sisters', longing more for secure emotional balance in relationship rather than assertiveness and raw power. Sadly, still too many males angle for power without realizing that emotional balance, and the associated ethical sensitivity, need also to be on their agenda if they are to match power with responsibly.

For too many people, marriage and cohabitation have become arenas of great disappointment, and of strong yet poorly managed emotion. There is, without doubt, excessive breakdown of relations between the sexes, and this frequently spills over into areas of child development and security. We have to find better ways forward. Emotional literacy is therefore crucial. The approach here has been to emphasize shared foundations, without being blind to the many rich and varied differences in gender behavior that both males and females need to learn to handle more adeptly.

9
TECHNIQUES FOR MANAGING FEELING STATES

9
TECHNIQUES FOR MANAGING FEELING STATES

'If you are patient in one moment of anger,
you will escape one hundred days of sorrow.'
Chinese proverb.
'Intelligent action results from a harmonious blend of emotion and reason.'
Adam Smith, 1722-1790
'When we have an emotion, we alter the state of the body in a variety of
ways, and then we register the resulting changes in the brain's body maps,
and feel the emotions. Emotions come first, feelings second.'
Antonio Damasio, 2003

'No emotional crisis is wholly the product of outward circumstances.'
Anon

For most of us, handling our emotions well involves a great deal of patience, self understanding, and at least an awareness of a few techniques that can be drawn upon in tight corners of emotional stress. This chapter outlines some emotional management techniques that help the cortex to get more of a grip on the heat of the heart, and thereby to minimize hurt. Working through at least some of the practical exercises here is likely to be of help.

9.1 A challenging management task

Our emotional sensors become embroidered with life experience, both at home and in the wider world. This, in combination with the character of our intimate nurture, determines the intensity, expression and handling capacities of the innate and learned emotions that we experience in each new life situation. Where basic nurture has been less than adequate, good emotional management tends to be all the more difficult. Everyone can improve the handling of their own emotions and their reactions to other people's emotions, and for most people intensive emotional therapy is not necessary. As we shall see, we need at least to be prepared to consider that emotional management is, in part at least, what we might call a 'spiritual discipline'. Without considering here particular propositions of religious faith, many people find that they can experience strengths beyond their immediate selves that may be drawn upon in circumstances of emotional and also ethical challenge.

The effective management of our feelings and emotions depends upon many factors. Consciousness and rationality, for the most part, are at the tip of the mental iceberg. Emotions happen to us; they are not experiences that we make happen. The make-up of our brains means that we cannot fake them. Our direct conscious controls upon our emotional life are weak, for, as we saw in chapter 3, the 'wiring' in the brain favors emotion, so that our thinking parts often fight a generally losing battle to banish emotions. Our feelings always want everything in place at once, and yet they are unreliable, rather like the weather! Hence getting more of a management grip on our emotions is both desirable, yet no simple task.

When we try to manipulate our emotions, that is, endeavor to *manage* them, we can only do so indirectly. Essentially there are only *two routes* through which we can do this. Both of these routes are 'slow' in the sense that they *both involve reflection* and patience within the strategies, and a sufficient 'playing for time', taking some kind of 'time out'.

The first possibility is through changing our reasoned

understanding of our world; that is, *redefining our perceptions* of some aspects of what we regard as *reality*. This may involve some changes in our views about what is worth bothering with, and what is better left aside, that is some kind of shift in our values and priorities. Such upper-brain, cortical activity then has a knock-on effect upon our emotional reactions. In effect we shift some of our goalposts concerning what we might get excited or anxious about.

The second possibility is to endeavor to manipulate the situational 'furniture' of people and events of our outside world so as to modify any disadvantaging impacts, both practical and emotional, upon us. This implies that we might hold some sort of silent power and persuasiveness to change other people and circumstances. For all of us, including prime ministers, princes or prelates, such capabilities are in practice quite limited, even though people with less formal status can sometimes feel unnecessarily intimidated by others who seem in control. Prime ministers cannot control the global economy; princes cannot demand that they be loved, and prelates, including the Pope, cannot control church members!

I once had a boss with whom eventually I had a good relationship, even though he got very angry with me almost on my first day of duty, losing his temper over my family friendly decision to live 50 miles away from headquarters. At that time I guess that he erroneously feared that I might be someone less committed than he to the institution, even though he had chaired my appointment's committee. Shortly after his angry outburst, my retired predecessor told me that such 'throwing of toys' events were normal, and almost a deliberate test of staff resilience. He advised me that the next time that I had to see my boss I should imagine him just in his underpants, just a man like me! That advice helped me to manipulate my perception of the situational furniture, and thereafter I felt much more confident in our private and committee meetings.

9.2 Basic rules of emotional engagement; protection from projection

There are essentially three interlocking rules to help us to handle our feelings and emotions in a grown-up way.

We must first understand that even though, as we have seen in chapters 5 and 6, all humans have basically the same framework of emotions, our feelings and emotions belong to us as individuals, and to nobody else. Whatever our state of being, whether pleasant or painful, emotions are a part of us; no less than our hands and feet or ears and noses. Therefore nobody other than our selves can be responsible for managing these emotions, except in the special cases of drug-related therapies that are chemically designed either to modify or to attenuate feeling states.

So basic *Rule 1* concerns *ownership:*

> *My feelings and emotions are mine. I must seriously accept them as a start towards handling or modifying them.*

The *second rule* arises from the phenomenon of *projection*. If we try to transfer or to dump our feelings, usually the painful ones, upon other people, we are essentially endeavoring to make them become responsible for ourselves having these feelings. This trait and bad habit, at margins of our awareness, is generally unproductive for human relationships. The process is called projection, and is a very common feature in human social behaviors. Here are five examples of projection through speech between two people:

a) 'You never listen.' … meaning essentially: 'I never feel heard.'

b) 'She kept me talking for half an hour.' … meaning: 'I allowed her to extend the telephone call for half an hour.'

c) 'The dog has really missed me while I have been away.' … meaning: 'I have missed the dog over the break.'

d) 'You are so ungrateful.' … meaning: 'I feel very hurt because you have not told me that you appreciate what I did just for you.'

e) 'You always clock-watch way ahead of going places.' … meaning: 'I feel irritated, even angry, over your anxiety about time, and your fears about being late. I just feel like staying at home on my own instead of going out with you.'

In respects, projection is a natural defense mechanism (see later section 10.5), even though not a particularly attractive one. Sometimes our consciousness would prefer others to carry our emotional burdens, but much more often projection is an unconscious reaction. This is not, however, in any way to deny that the acts of others do sometimes hurt us emotionally, bringing into our consciousness, and sometimes physiology (such as intestinal cramp), deeply painful feelings. The capacity to wound others' feelings, and to be wounded emotionally by others is not in doubt. But the responses made do involve choice, given the exercise of reflective capacity.

So basic **Rule 2** concerns **responsibility**:

> *It is not helpful for me, whether in thought or in action, to try to make others responsible for my feelings. Others are responsible for what they feel, do or say. I am responsible for handling my feelings associated with what others do or say to me.*

The third rule concerns active listening. When we are listening to and interacting with others we may hear about, or feel intuitively, their emotions. It is not however necessary for us to acquire those same emotions, even if they seem to be being forced upon us by projection. A good listener fully accepts as 'fact' the emotions of others, but does not have to receive them as a kind of unwanted personal gift.

So basic **Rule 3** concerns **empathetic listening**:

> *We must be attuned to and recognize other people's emotions; neither making them our own, nor accepting responsibility for them.*

An example of a brief domestic conversation is now given in order to illustrate these three basic rules of feelings management.

Gill says: *'You did not tidy your room John. You are so inconsiderate.'*

There are two mature alternatives for John in relation to this statement. First he can identify with Gill's feeling of annoyance, and, instead of becoming annoyed himself through being negatively labeled (from which an argument might develop), John might respond with the statement:

'You are annoyed because my room is still untidy.'

In this response John reflects back Gill's emotion to convey that he has heard it. Alternatively John can identify Gill's feeling as sadness, and respond by recognizing that, but not accepting responsibility for it. In this case John might say:

'Gill, you are disappointed that I have not tidied my room. I just did not think of it earlier.'

This acknowledges John's lack of malice and also Gill's negative feeling. In these two alternative responses John is managing his emotions more maturely than Gill and is putting into practice golden Rule 3. Alternatively the whole dialogue could have started quite differently, with less initial hostility from Gill as follows:

John, I have been thinking that you might tidy your room soon, for you have not done it for quite a while, and that tends to make me feel that you don't care for our home's tidiness.'

Given this opening gambit, John more easily recognizes Gill's feeling about sharing the chore of tidiness, and since Gill owns both her thoughts and feelings (practicing Rule 1) he has no temptation to be annoyed in return. In this case he might respond with:

'I am sorry that you are feeling that I am indifferent about tidiness. I do appreciate all you do, but have not thought about tidying my room recently. But now you mention it, the room is in a bit of a mess. My mind has been

on other things, including new job applications. I will see to it within the week.'

Here John empathizes with, though does not own Gill's feelings, for she does not imply that he should. He then gives Gill positive affirmation, and, promises to act. John owns what he has failed to do, and this is an example of practicing Rule 2, 'taking responsibility'.

All this may look rather labored as an analysis of a short verbal exchange, but clearly we all need practice in applying the three rules, particularly *the pause* inherent in good listening. The pause allows for both reflection upon and reflecting back an emotion to a speaker, thereby indicating that it has been registered. But the anguish avoided from an argument deflected is worth a great deal in daily life. Opening gambits in emotional signaling, whoever makes them in a conversation – and these may include a frown or a smile – are usually the most crucial in affecting outcome. The first response, whatever the initial signal is, however, no less crucial in avoiding an unproductive tangle, or worse.

Personal exercise 25

This exercise is in two parts.

Firstly, six statements are given that project the feelings of the speaker elsewhere. In your own words write for each statement what you think is really being said.

(a) You expect me to be in two places at once.

(b) He just ignores me, and then treats me like dirt.

(c) Silly 'red tape', that's all it is.

(d) You are a real male chauvinist.

(e) You dislike me for what I have done.

(f) You make me feel so angry that one day I shall explode.

Secondly, recall a recent argument or obvious interpersonal tension and track back as accurately as possible to what was said by you and the other person when it began. Write the key opening phrases of what was said, followed by a re-run of the early script that reflects the spirit of the three rules given in this section.

Arising from the three basic rules outlined in this section are **two practical guides for feelings management expressed as follows:**

- **In sequence:** *'Listen to the feeling. Name the feeling. Own the feeling. Tame and aim the feeling. Review the feeling.'*

- **Time-aware:** *'Always, and in all ways, endeavor to play for time.' Cultivate the precious and potent pause, so facilitating at least some reflective decisions.*

9.3 Tracking and managing difficult feelings

Having noted basic aspects of brain science, it is clear that when sufficient of our neural brain circuits 'get in line', with neurons acting in a unison of flow, capability is just around the corner in the form of skills, insights, and creativity. The last of these may involve 'lateral thinking' through which we have the confidence to experiment, being ready to challenge existing ideas, orthodoxies and limiting views of reality. Sometimes we can punish ourselves emotionally from our own blinkered perceptions. Likewise, when our brain circuits move out of synchronicity, we become 'up-tight' and experience emotional turbulence, and this diminishes our immediate capabilities, poise and creativity. As emotional stressors increase, performance tends to decrease.

At the very least, a properly reflective attitude helps people to recognize when their poise and rationality could be on the verge of being hi-jacked by their limbic system's *amygdala* (see chapter 3), so becoming out of control, or 'losing it' as people now say. No less, a reflective facial countenance fosters our empathy for others. This can help us to pick up on early-warning signs of irritability, frustration or anxiety amongst people close by so as to prevent them having a downer or lose control of themselves. Always it is much more difficult for us to tune into others' emotional states if our own are unsettled, for our psychic energy is no less finite than our physical energy.

Personal exercise 26

Imagine yourself in each of the six situations now outlined. Note for each:
- *Changes of feelings in you that seem likely to arise*
- *Any likely associated physiological reactions (e.g. perspiring, smiling), and*
- *What the principle of reflective, 'playing for time' over emotional management tells you to do.*
    1. *You win a prize in a raffle, but knock your hip on a table when going forward to collect it.*
    2. *Someone who is supposed to be doing something urgent for you is staring into space.*
    3. *You are smacked on the face.*
    4. *Your faithful pet dies suddenly.*
    5. *You hear screams from an open patch of land on a dark night.*
    6. *You are waiting for a loved one. It is now 20 minutes past rendezvous time.*

Becoming more reflective about our feelings does not imply that we should dwell upon them incessantly, whether in their constancy or in their capriciousness. It is also counterproductive for us to expect to feel in specific ways, and then get fed up with ourselves if we don't! Some days most people get out of bed feeling lethargic for no apparent reason, and there is no point in feeling guilty or irritable about such a feeling; one just has to 'stay with it', and, sure enough, it will almost certainly disappear. On other days we may feel 'on edge' when we want to be relaxed. Trying to relax is usually a dead-end activity; there may be a need for a calming 'grace', and that medium cannot be willed, only waited for in trust. One of our biggest needs is to have faith that our past, present and future journey is not going to be wasted.

9.4 Balance of feeling, and feelings in the balance

We have already encountered, particularly in chapters 5 and 6, both the positive and negative elements within some emotions. We now examine illustrations of balance between conflicting feelings in particular practical situations.

For example, using a five-point analysis, let us unpack a familiar case of sensitivity to criticism. Tom, a quietly conscientious man, in a reflective moment, notices that whenever his work is criticized, he swiftly feels very hostile to the critic.

Analysis of Tom's inner observation

1   *Trigger:* criticism, possibly quite fair and not malicious.
2   *Overall feeling state:* hostility and hurt.
3   *Associated feelings:* personal pride and esteem, insecurity, wounding, anger.
4   *Plus option:* facing the reality of imperfect work, and the will to improve.
5   *Minus option:* hostility to critic, further self-wounding by non-cooperation.

The next personal exercise gives practice in the parallel analysis of four similar individual reflections that suggest emotional review.

Personal exercise 27

Follow the 5-point analysis just given for each of the following four examples:

- Alan notices that he is becoming very anxious about the sale of his house.

- Patricia notices that she has become bored with being a school governor.
- Nigel notices he cannot bear to see sights of suffering children on TV.
- Kirsty notices that she is completely indifferent to sports results.

Finally do the same kind of analysis for one or two of your own reflective 'noticing' of feelings concerning aspects of your own life.

Having a mixture of feelings and emotions, and weighing them up, is in fact quite common for all of us. We can experience thereby a kind of *emotional seesaw.* For example, we may be really happy that our sports team won, yet immediately afterwards rather sad for the opposition because they helped to make a really good game and were dignified in defeat. Other examples of emotional seesaws might be:

- 'I am torn between being excited about my new job, and being apprehensive that I might not come up to scratch for my new employer'.
- 'I am torn between being furious that his bad driving damaged my car, and relief that I have no broken bones'.
- 'I am torn between being lost without my dear mother, but glad that she is no longer in such pain'.

Being 'torn between' emotions can be quite an inner tussle. For example, in the case of waiting for someone who is late to meet you, or perhaps late for a meal you have cooked, the following 'battle of balance' might go on inside your head:

- *Basic emotional state* is one of *anxiety* and *rejection.* 'You have not turned up. Late as usual. I feel so unimportant to you, and again simply abandoned'.
- *The internal 'parental' authority of reason and conscience.* 'There is no point in being anxious; it makes no difference whatever, and he always turns up eventually ... Anyway, I'm not bothered about being here alone. People waste so much time and energy getting anxious and worrying, and mostly

its usually all so pointless because many, even most things do turn out OK'.

- *Idealized safe image of presentation to the world.* 'It is his life, and I am quite OK. I do not fret about things, for that is stupid and a waste of energy'.

When 'he' does eventually turn up, nobody can predict which of these responses in the balance will win through. When we pause, and give opportunity to rehearse our important opening gambit, at least we get in touch with reason and choice!

9.5 Management energy beyond ourselves

It is a fact of pastoral experience that many people find that emotions cannot be properly managed or handled without reference to spirituality. This is a dimension of being and resourcefulness that pops up from the unconscious, seemingly beyond the tangible self, and yet nonetheless intimately intertwined with it. This dimension of a 'sixth sense' resource tends to come to our aid when we least expect it.

In some religious traditions, or more local cultural interpretations of them, emotions are still seen as irrelevant and possibly, like sexuality, dangerous, as if religious faith is to be seen to lie beyond emotional life or even superior to it. There is even fear that divine messages delivered with emotion and that confront our emotions, tend to harm, as if we are required suddenly to discard sense and reason in any awakening. In fact most sacred texts, including the Bible, grapple throughout with emotional questions. In addition, the many reports concerning the spiritual and godly becoming a reality for people, past and present, their whole lives, and very much their emotions, are involved and climb on board the journey of faith.

Secular materialistic humanism implies more or less the same, and reduces all feelings and emotions to transient electric charges and biochemical reactions that we deal with best by almost ignoring them as merely temporary disturbances to rationality. In view of what was examined in chapter 3, this is bad science, no less than religious escapes from the emotional heart of matters being bad theology.

Our innate and learned emotions unavoidably keep coming back at us, along with associated feelings. They are not some external visitation, but part of who we are in nature. We can often 'resurrect' particular feelings or moods from within, by thinking back into situations that were powerful at the time, or passing a place where a striking event took place such as an accident, a death, a falling in love. Thus, emotions are a part of our essential being, part of our essence, our mortal and perhaps immortal spirit, and certainly not separate from our reality.

There is a wealth of spiritual literature that examines emotions helpfully. Little of this has been undermined by the very much later arrival on the map of human knowledge of modern psychology and psychiatry in the quest of understanding people. Some of the spiritual deposit grows from monastic traditions, Christian and other, which have wrestled with problems of inner human nature more than any other. We modern people have too little sense of intellectual and spiritual history, yet the apparent irrationality and destructiveness of some of our emotions continues to dog much of our aspired progress. Fortunately, we do not have to rediscover spiritual disciplines from scratch.

For example, John Cassian (AD 360-435) tells of the importance of 'naming our demons', by which he meant negative emotions and not 'evil spirits'. He advised discoursing with these, facing them square in the face, as a means of reducing their intensity and avoiding debilitating depressions suffered by (amongst many others) the prophet Job. St. Augustine of Hippo's *Confessions* (AD 354-430) reflect the mind and heart of a harassed seeker of the truth, and a man of fallible passions like our own, which can touch us with a ring of truth, encountering our common, frail humanity. The psalms also contain a great deal of insight into raw emotions and spiritual ways of dealing with them. Controlled 'fantasy journeys', in which we are taken sensitively by a leader upon imagination-stretching routes, can also illuminate the inner life.

The chief 'emotional management tools' within the spiritual dimension are contemplation and prayer that engage practically with individuals' inner reality. These means of calming our 'demons' of negative emotionality release what can only be called 'the gift of grace'. This has been an aspect of my story that I have experienced as a scientist on many occasions when, beyond mid-life, I have found the wisdom of being truly quiet and emptied of pressing thoughts and tasks. This is not religious sentimentality, but human reality, when given a chance, grace being elusive if time rush, ego and distractions dominate.

Features of *spiritual channelling* may be summarised as follows:

The channel of **prayer**	*Features of quiet gifts of natural* **grace**
Opening up ourselves to the divine.	Assistance from the beyond arrives within
Patiently listening to the inner voice.	a gift or state of peace, and of belonging.
Quiet contemplation or meditation.	A calm sense of awe and thanksgiving.
Filtering requests, pleas, hopes.	Goodwill, favor, bestowing honor.
Giving thanks and praise for life.	Relief of a burden or stress.

Should we feel pressures that awaken concern to face our selves holistically, encounters with the spiritual, the 'numinous' and 'divine possibilities' are likely. Here are two illustrative accounts of this kind of encounter, too rarely spoken of in our mechanized, shrunken universe.

John's story

My wife and I sometimes have really bad rows. Something small and basically trivial starts them off, usually when we've been too busy or have just got overtired. Then we throw two-way insults and hurts, some from long ago. The row just escalates, as if literally we are both driven to dump some sort of inner poison on each other. It is very unpleasant, and we've got very close to violence and have thrown things like cushions and dishcloths. Most people don't know of course, thank God; only the children, sadly, who are occasionally within earshot. We're not proud of ourselves about this of course. However, we've both noticed that when we've let go all we can, as though there's nothing worse to say, a sort of calm relief comes after the storm. It seems to come from beyond our pain and hassle. Its as though someone else has heard our cries and just says 'I hear what you feel. Its awful, but its OK, and you can feel better now.' Then we find we can say we're sorry, and we make up always within a few hours. It's hell while it lasts, but new life always comes again. It is like a power beyond us that cleans up our emotional mess. 'Amazing grace' my wife calls it (after the hymn of that name, written by John Newton, 1725-1807). I guess we all need grace sometimes, and grace is always hiding somewhere. Well not actually hiding, just waiting for me to pause to touch again the inward parts of my reality that I tend to ignore.

Peter's story

I am a rather ambitious sort of person because I want things to go well, especially for me. What people think of me is very important. Well, I had one or two setbacks. My school results were not good enough to get me into the university degree course in Business Finance that I wanted. Then Dad's own small business went into recession and that blocked off another opening for me. I got into quite a panic about my career and whole future. Life just seemed like a rat race and I wasn't up to speed. Dad had sort of made it, without much formal education, but the recession wasn't his fault. The whole situation was just one long worry. Even my girlfriend Pat was finding me a bore because I had no sense of direction, let alone a sense of humor. Then one day I took a walk by myself over the moors and down into the next valley by the river estuary, and I heard a voice ask me: 'Is it now time for you to stop trying to run your own life in this very anxious way, anxiously worrying to no effect? Sort out those things you can and must change; then leave the rest in my hands.'

I still can't decide whether this was my 'inner voice' or some 'divine voice'; perhaps the two are really the same? And, by the way, I do not much like the word 'God'. In English it sounds harsh and clipped, so feels not very friendly. For me no god is worth having unless he, she or it is friendly, mostly on my side. After I had listened that day by the river I felt a whole lot better, as if there was another friend around who knew what I was feeling. Now I ask this voice, with its good pair of ears, into my situation much more often, and any panic always goes. It feels like a little miracle that restores my poise and sense of direction. Pat has always said her prayers, so we talk about this now and have got a whole lot closer. I tell her, though, it's more than just saying prayers; it's listening out for the inner voice of a friend 'Big Ears'. I think its good to think of God as having big ears – like an old, wise and strong elephant. Pat reckons our friend has big arms and shoulders too, to hug, comfort and even carry us when we are worn out; and, typical woman, her god has plenty of boxes of tissues to dry peoples' tears. For me this inner friend has become my 'appliance of spiritual science' and I guess that's what all those ancient saints and prophets were in touch with.

We will be returning to some further issues of spiritual development in chapter 12. Meanwhile, the following five practical meditation guidelines for feelings management are adapted from St Ignatius Loyola (1491-1556).

Guidelines for meditation on feelings

1. Direct your core being, your essence, towards the Creator beheld as both perfect love and perfect acceptance. Hold that sense of presence without rush.
2. Let go of anxieties, one by one, and share each of your fears by facing them and naming them.
3. Examine both creative moods and feelings, and destructive moods and feelings, not according to pleasure or pain, but

according to their effects upon you and others.

4. Label those moods and feelings that draw you towards the Divine Love as 'consolations', comforting your soul. Also label those that tend to turn you away from such love and experienced as 'desolations'. (Desolations pass, and can be creative if we act towards such periods of pain without distractions of anger, and in faith.)

5. Pray and hope for less desolation. Never go back in desolation upon a decision made in a time of consolation, for the original decision will have been close to love's reliability, goodness and truth, for consolations are close to deep truth.

9.6 Consequences of relational-emotional management

Although our emotional structure is arguably the least plastic aspect of the brain, much seeming to be centered within the limbic system, the strong evidence from prompting the cortex's active involvement shows an amazing capacity for new learning, given opportunity.

The spectrum of consequences of learning to manage our relational and emotional lives has been well summarized by Daniel Goleman, and are adapted here as the following list:

Emotional self-awareness
- Improved recognition and naming of one's own emotions.
- More able to understand causes of feelings.
- Recognize the difference between feelings and actions.

Managing emotions
- Increased thresholds of frustration, with active anger management.

- Reduced social disruption, and fighting and aggression.
- More positive feelings about self, community and family.
- Less loneliness and social anxiety.

Productive harnessing of emotions

- Reduced impulsiveness, increased self-control and responsibility.
- Greater focus on the particular task in hand.
- Improved educational achievement.

Empathetic reading of others emotions

- More able to take another person's perspective.
- Improved listening to others.

Handling relationships

- Improved conflict resolution and communication skills.
- More involved with and sought out by peers.
- More concerned, considerate and democratic in dealing with others.
- Better group member and problem solver.

Adapted from *Emotional Intelligence,* 1995, pages 283-4

So we can say for certain that improved self and emotional awareness, through developing the reflective arts, helps people to live more constructively on the inside with themselves, and also to relate better to other people. Included here is the ability to influence events, to provide effective service, and to work in teams at home, in employment, and in voluntary community activities of all kinds.

We now move to examine human feelings in relation to social values, conscience, trust, and group behavior, matters that lie at the interface between individuals and their wider society.

10
FEELINGS, SOCIAL VALUES, CONSCIENCE AND TRUST

10
FEELINGS, SOCIAL VALUES, CONSCIENCE AND TRUST

'No heart is pure that is not passionate, no virtue safe that is not enthusiastic';
(and enthusiasm means literally 'divinity within').'
Soren Kierkegaard, 1813-55

'The contents of the personal ... are feeling-toned.
The contents of the collective unconscious are known as archetypes'.
Carl Jung, 1875-1961

'A crowd, whether it be a dangerous mob or an amiably joyous gathering at a picnic, is not a community. It has a mind, but no institutions, no organization, no coherent unity, no history, no traditions'.

Josiah Royce, 1855-1916, in *The Problem of Christianity*

We experience and feel emotionality individually, and have here encountered (in sections 2.5 and 4.5) the interactions between our emotions and our personal values. In this chapter we take that a stage further to consider feelings and emotions in relation to social issues, and to examine associated matters concerning both conscience and social trust.

10.1 Feelings about social issues

Aspects of justice, race, gender, sexuality, religion, law and order, politics and morality are all very fertile territory for our feelings and emotions. Frequently, as the media remind us in every news bulletin, such topics easily prompt unhelpful conflict and intolerance between individuals and groups that relate to our strongly held values and beliefs. Here we encounter again links between personal values and emotions, and we need to recognize that some of our values may be based upon false perceptions and beliefs concerning those whose cultural ways are strange to us. This may lead to prejudices that whip up hostile feelings derived from exaggerated fears and threats unhelpful to social harmony.

Ill-informed prejudice in the arenas of race, gender, religion, politics and ethics, in particular, can prompt dangerous passions. The first exercise in this chapter is designed to prompt personal review of feelings about these kinds of social issues.

Personal exercise 28

Use a table as shown in order to review your emotions concerning two examples in each of five broad social issues. The table first requires words for feelings and emotions (but not opinions), triggered in you for each of the 10 examples. Then follows your opinions for each example using one of the three categories shown. Finally, for each of the ten topics, note your reflective views concerning your personal need, or otherwise, for a greater tolerance.

Social issues examples	My feelings and emotions	My opinion of topic: OK/ not OK /uncertain	My need for more tolerance? Yes/No
A. *Gender.* 1. Women's rugby 2. Paternity leave			
B. *Race and ethnicity.* 1. Gypsy campsite 2. Black bride, white groom			
C. *Religion.* 1. The Pope 2. An Islamic 'fatwa'			
D. *Politics.* 1. European currency 2. Immigration			
E. *Ethical matters.* 1. Abortion on demand 2. Rural and urban litter			

Finally, reflect upon your 'need for tolerance total score' (range zero to 10) arising from scoring 1 or 0 for each example, and make a note about how you see tolerance relating to both truth and your style of expressing feelings about social questions.

10.2 Values and conscience

Our personal values are, as we have noted, a varied mix of issues, traits, activities and things that matter to us as individuals, reflecting the particular characteristics of our lives. While values may be described by language, they are illustrated by behavior. Others tend to make judgments about us mostly from our behavior, so if we 'talk values' (as do teachers, politicians, priests, police and others) we are properly expected to 'walk values'. Involved here are matters of integrity and conscience.

We derive our values from a mix of *sources*, primarily:

- *revealed* authority, from holy texts, religious and local 'tribal' traditions;
- *imposed* authority, such as civil law, military doctrine, and school discipline;
- *chosen* authority through voluntary group memberships: such as church, sports club, town council, professional association, gang;
- *academic* related authority in various disciplines;
- *subversive* 'authorities', such as distorted images (some from the mass media), virtual realities, and
- *family* values acquired formally and informally, but not necessarily without rebellion, from those who bring us up from infancy to the adult stage.

Most, if not all of our values have a relational component, with the focus on self, others, goods and chattels, social and physical environments and, for some, God. Values are not inborn, though the environment that chance bestows upon us at birth and in infancy, and then beyond (when our own choices come much more into play), is littered with implicit and explicit values. So our values become interlinked with our emerging life story, appearing as central to what defines us, or, in other words, our 'identity'.

When our values are challenged, under threat or even coercively violated, our emotions are understandably aroused, being close to our 'passion centre'. Values hover near to the 'heart' of the person, close to our motivation and 'action energy', acting as some kind of 'emotional guardian' that gives the heart its reasons. All this interacts with each person's conscience and its inner tussles with ethics and virtue, for moral life in some shape or form is inescapable for everyone.

Explicitly linking ethics with emotions, the dictionary defines *conscience* as 'the moral sense of right and wrong, especially as felt by a person and affecting his or her behavior'. *Conscience is an inner voice* triggered when moral choice encounters the temptation to deviate from what is felt and/or known to be right. It interacts with emotions, and usually predicts uneasy feelings, regret and guilt when not heeded. Conscience thus seeks to be heard and considered, confronting us with a sense of responsibility for our own actions, and the fact that actions have consequences. While conscience is very likely to be concerned with civic laws and sanctions, it is rarely merely dictated by them, being influenced by those close to us, including peers, upbringing, mentors, heroes, and by education. It is not inherently primed to be static or unchanging, and may become further sensitized through captivating stories having ethical challenge, learning from mistaken personal decisions, and reflecting upon experiences of love, pain and loss.

Conscience tells us that to seek after virtue, rather than vice, is both reasonable, and indeed an aspect of rational self-interest in constructing a 'good life'. Our *emotions help to prime the moral universe and underpin much, if not all our moral, or immoral, behavior*. Such reason as we might apply to moral situations cannot be segregated from our emotional sub-structure. One practical consequence of this is that the moral capacities of children and adults are not best served by simply forcing on them 'do and don't commandments', unless these are explained alongside a considerate emotional environment. As noted previously, we *become moral through being treated with consideration*, crucially by having our emotions respected and cared for at least over our first twenty years of life.

Personal exercise 29

Reflect upon one incident in your life in which you acted against your conscience, and record the emotional consequences for you that perhaps nobody else saw or even realized. Now note a recent ethical dilemma or battle of conscience where the inner voice won out, and the associated feelings.

10.3 The unconscious and the shadow self

This book about e-motions has no choice but to speak to your conscious mind. But there is a paradox, because everyone has a vast unconscious area of neurological life that includes dreams, fantasies, wishes and memories, some of which are repressed or censured by the rational part of conscience. The 'unconscious' is an area explored particularly within the traditions of psychoanalysis, a discipline that seeks to understand and manage, even heal, extremes of emotion, in particular those that are so disturbed as to severely impair quality of life. The human unconscious is thought to account for a memory store significantly greater than the conscious. It is awesome to recognize that perhaps two thirds of whom we really are, in terms of brain capacity, is submerged in a living mystery!

The boundary between our conscious and unconscious is not static, nor linear, and both parts contain both emotional and reasoned material. Diagram 11 depicts this interface, and also indicates the associated ideas of our visible public persona and the invisible private self.

Diagram 11: A depiction of the boundary between the human conscious and unconscious

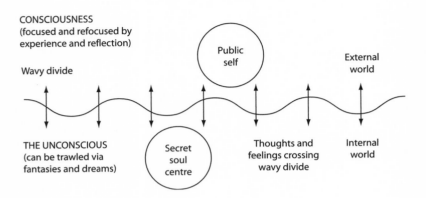

Within such a picture the whole self is a combination of the public self, the conscious private self (that which we know in secret) and the unconscious (that of which we are not immediately aware). Embedded somewhere, and often unawares, is our deepest inner centre, that some call the 'secret soul centre'. Many down the ages have reported that this soul centre becomes more accessible through the disciplines of contemplation, meditation and prayer.

Swiss psychiatrist, Carl Jung (1875-1961), extended the idea of the 'personal unconscious', sensed in mystical writings down many centuries, to that of the *'collective unconscious'* for which there is evidence in synchronicities ('coincidental' happenings having meaning in our lives but which defy chance), in ancestral resonance, and of course the commonalities we have noted in human emotional structure. In the collective unconscious (that Jung saw as compatible with an archetypal 'First Cause' of love as association) we have a sense of universal connectedness with the evolved spirits of our species. This is to hypothesize that we are most deeply joined one with another, past, present and future, through our unconscious, and through a range of universal signs, symbols, patterns and myths for which there is ample cross-cultural evidence. Such an idea links with a range of religious experience recorded within the major world faiths. Now emerging are fascinating new possibilities arising from links between neurosciences, biology, psychology, sub-particle physics, philosophy and religion that underscore life as a meaningful adventure.

The light and shade in the human personality has been known for millennia, and is an aspect of both mood and conscience. Jung termed our darker side the 'shadow self', and saw this as largely unconscious traits of personality that the conscious ego tends to ignore, reject or deny. Like any physical object caught in the light, we may project our shadow onto others in our path, so perceiving them as people partly akin to our denied image, unable to see them as they really are. Mastering these issues of taking rather than projecting responsibility is the task of integration of a holistic awareness of the self. This requires sustaining a comfortable enough balance of ego with shadow, of masculine with feminine traits, and of our past history and story with the active present. This Jung termed 'individuation', in reality a courageous inner process that, if addressed at all, tends to be deferred until the second half of life.

10.4 One in a crowd?

Because we are social beings, our experience of emotions within group situations are often different from those we feel when we are alone or with just one other person. We may combine 'in spirit' with others to form what may be called 'corporate emotions', experienced in family, crowd and group behavior, in professional and consumer activities, and over political and artistic preferences.

Crowds in particular can arouse strong emotions, as we know particularly at events such as football matches or civic functions such as receptions, degree ceremonies, or particular major national events. In these, a potential amplification of some emotions by 'herd instinct' may be counterbalanced by other defensive reactions that reflect a fear of domination by 'the herd', such as more regularly happens within peer groups. Other particular examples of corporate emotions are found at family 'life markers' such as weddings and funerals, music concerts, the variety of events in sports stadiums, or at political or evangelistic rallies. This is not to imply however that all those present at such events share the same feelings; indeed some may feel embarrassed and uncomfortable of presence, perhaps attending out of a sense of duty.

It is important that we learn to monitor our emotions when we are in group situations, recognizing that not far from any crowd lies space and solitude wherein personal emotions can more readily be recognized and reviewed. The next exercise provides an opportunity to reflect on personal reactions in some crowded environments.

Personal exercise 30

Use the tabular format shown for recording personal reactions envisaged in each of the six situations listed.

Real-life situation	Feelings and emotions roused	Actions suggested by feelings aroused
1. Stuck in a motorway traffic jam.		
2. Swimming in a crowded pool.		
3. In a full theatre when fire alarms go off.		
4. Disturbed at a quiet scenic viewpoint by two coachloads of tourists.		
5. Having big cases on a cramped train.		
6. Jostled within a crowd emptying from a football stadium after a match.		

10.5 Projection as a defense mechanism

We have noted that the ways in which we relate to each other, and to the world around us, are influenced greatly by our personal unconscious, that part of ourselves which contains buried and forgotten memories, imaginings and feelings. The repression of painful or socially taboo thoughts, feelings and impulses is an aspect of our *defense mechanisms* that assist us in the maintenance of boundaries of living.

Repressed emotions may lead to compensatory reactions in behavior style. For example, an inner sense of despair may reveal itself in some people as a compulsive optimism; a sense of low worth can prompt strivings to be recognized; distrust of parents, amid a sense of duty towards them, may prompt idealizations of their reliability; and longings for attention may appear as excessive self-effacement. Living in and by denials of this sort saps relational energy within inner struggles of personality.

Another aspect of repressed emotions links with the concept of *projection*, outlined in section 9.2, and also associated with our prejudices. Psychological projection includes a diversionary tactic of the ego to prevent inner self-knowledge, so keeping our shadows in their place in the subconscious. In projection we tend to transfer traits that our conscious finds unacceptable within ourselves by projecting them onto other people, or organizations such as workplaces, sectors of government, clubs or churches. Projection is a very powerful defense mechanism and *avoids our taking responsibility for at least some of our own unacceptable dispositions,* for example a lack of patience or perception (see Rule 2 in section 9.2, page 180).

The accompanying danger of projection is that the person offloading the unacceptable emotion feels on the side of the righteous, on the moral high ground, the other person or institution being seen as basically bad and definitely at fault. Religious and other people who sense that they bask in the pure light of revelation are particularly prone to this besetting sin. Failing to embrace their shadow, they tend to become over-assured of their insights, piety or doctrinal veracity. In Christ's time this tendency was strongly evident in the behavior of the Pharisees, and now, two millennia later, too prevalent in churches that were founded on the single principle of an incarnate Divine embrace of love and friendship without conditions.

Uninvolved observers are more easily aware of our emotional blindness when we engage in projection, and they may consequently come to mistrust our judgment and lose respect for us. This can make the person doing the projecting feel isolated, prompting a strengthening of the projection, so making matters worse. People who are insecure and not coping well with life, are more likely to fall victim to projection than secure, loved and happy people, but all of us project sometimes in some situations.

A genuine relationship with another person can happen only when both are prepared to face the negative sides of their inner selves and the associated feelings, confronting personal shadow material. Such close scrutiny of oneself requires courage. The personal recognition of projection Jung termed 'a moral achievement beyond the ordinary'. Yet only when false illusions of the self are stripped away can we see others for who they truly are, and become free to see other realities more faithfully.

A positive aspect of projection does however need noting. Our attraction to heroes, and the idealisms that they often embody, can be inspiring. Mentors and role models, often powerful amongst the young, can assist us to reach out beyond ourselves, and so extend our present achievements, making more of our inherent possibilities. Effective youth workers, for example, are adept at handling young people's negative projections concerning authority, by staying calm amid truculent complaints, and certainly not taking these personally. Such mentors help their charges to develop their inner will, sense of agency and responsibility.

10.6 Projections within social groups

Projection is a widespread feature within the relational fabric of societies. A few more instances of the phenomenon are noted here before returning to matters of social trust.

Socially almost all of us are affiliated to three basic kinds of social group.

Primary groups: small in size, no more than 12–15 persons, with each in various ways inter-dependent, as in family groups, with perhaps a few 'informally adopted'. A tutorial, workshop-seminar or pastoral support group may also, at least for a period, develop characteristics of a supportive family.

Secondary groups: medium in size, maybe from about 15–500, having explicit functions. These groups embody little personal intimacy, and can still perform with little overall change if we cease to be active members, if, for example, we are on holiday or even resign. Examples are professional bodies, schools, a university department, sports clubs, church congregations and employment settings.

Tertiary groups: large or very large in size, from above about 500–millions, such as in nationality or ethnicity, or other broad identity definers by religion or political party. These groups have a permanence, yet tend to attract our serious commitment in membership as need arises rather than on a regular basis.

The phenomenon of projection is variously displayed in each of these three broadly applicable group settings.

In family life, particularly among partners where the maintenance of emotional intimacy presents ongoing challenges, a tendency to blame the other for all of one's own bad feelings is common. In extended families, individuals may be used as a scapegoat for wider deficiencies, a feature also prevalent in other groups that have some form of care remit. In schools there may be scapegoats in particular lessons, tutor groups, games teams or dormitories. Problems in voluntary societies and clubs also prompt projection if members prefer not to examine their own roles within difficulties that have corporate responsibility. Some small family type groups make take out their spite on innocent outsiders because stresses cannot be safely resolved within the group. For example, a husband who does not negotiate well with his wife might unconsciously take out his frustration on a colleague at work, or lash out at the family dog. Or an apparently cooperative student, hiding frustrations over school or college procedure, may project an exaggerated authoritarianism onto parents.

Safe psychological climates within institutions, government departments, businesses, charities, schools, hospitals and other care facilities are vital for their daily effectiveness. The tone of an organization is set by past and present leadership, not only in terms of technical and professional skills but, crucially, through the genuineness, psychological maturity and integrity of key managers. This demands that each manager sees their role as more corporate than personal, with egos reasonably in check. Staff morale, trust and commitment, whatever the market or budget circumstances, are central to the maintenance, growth and indeed recovery of enterprises. Inconsiderate approaches to these issues are generally unwise, counterproductive and often unethical. Yet psychological disregard for and manipulation of workforces remains commonplace, despite the growth of Business Studies and seductive mission statements. In restructuring companies or public institutions trust often becomes threadbare, with high, rarely quantified performance costs. The emergent culture of litigation, creates defensive maneuvers of individual self-interest, detrimental to team endeavor.

In any group there is plenty of scope for the inadequate person who copes by using projection as a defense mechanism. Such people, if also capable in other ways, tend to work themselves into positions of power without having enough associated personal responsibility. In short, good managers and leaders know their inner selves, both strengths and weaknesses. Yet their formation mostly leaves the inner dispositions to chance. It is also possible to sustain a position of emotional power without rising far in an institutional hierarchy. Performing an essential function that nobody else can or will do, gives personal power as a 'gatekeeper', promoting the belief that, without this operative, a segment of the institution would cease to function. I well remember in my first job that the chemicals storekeeper had become the most powerful employee in our department, the protection of 'his' stores almost more important than the service he was paid to deliver!

Personal adequacy is in various ways sustained by projection at others' expense, and challenging such traits in others requires considerable tact if cooperation and good relations are to be sustained within teams and management chains. Inadequate managers tend to project their own fears and uncertainties onto their staffs through over zealous attempts to control, thereby undermining the very trust upon which their worst fears are based. Organizational management by over-prescription of targets rarely gets the best out of people, and generally gives only temporary comfort to insecure layers in chains of command.

In politics and business the habit or 'craft' of projection may be used in a more refined, or even planned and sophisticated ways to denigrate others' policies or products. Those who have perfected this are often the ones more likely to gain power or a very good market share. The large group, party or nation to which one gives one's loyalty often becomes one that cannot admit publicly to its faults. For this reason, politicians and large organizations rarely apologize. Failures, even corruption, and certainly inefficiencies that are known to insiders, tend to be formally ignored, hushed up or projected externally.

Many political decisions and policies have a large emotional content and so are never totally rational. To understand them fully, the motivations and emotional issues that lie behind formal statements, including fear of loss of power, need to be recognized. One projection technique is to amplify the threat of 'the enemy'. The 'enemy' may be one of the internal team, perhaps a cabinet minister acting as fall guy in times of wavering public confidence, akin to the fate of professional football managers when their teams have a poor run of results. The political party lasting the longest may be that which seems most united because it is the most skilled in projecting its weaknesses onto its competitors through the mass media. During elections, political issues may be falsely polarized in order to provide more incentive to vote. Projection stirs up people emotionally to press choice amongst the many wavering voters. Parties may do well by placing far less emphasis on their own policies than suggesting that others' policies are a threat. Casting a vote with discernment is usually more an emotional than an ideological matter. An informed electorate needs to understand this as a part of safeguarding democracy, seeing the real issues beneath the hype and projections.

In international politics, wars have been started by nations who have projected some of their own insufficiently examined troubles onto other nations. It can be more comfortable to see an enemy beyond rather than an enemy within, while history shows that to rally forces to war is one way of creating national unity. Arguably, some countries have not perceived some of their own shadow material clearly enough in their diplomatic and military responses to shocking and unjustifiable terrorist attacks.

Much *advertising* aims to make people buy products, and takes psychology into account, using projection as a tool. The projection is aimed at the psychological malleability of those to whom the product is being targeted. Our emotional needs are exploited by subtle and less than subtle seductions that may bypass our analytic and reflective processes. The exploitation of personal doubts and weaknesses can be seen in a variety of examples. Fears about lack of personal sophistication are played upon in adverts for perfumes, beer, state-of-the-art cars, designer fashions and all manner of technical equipment. Adverts promoting expensive cleaners and disinfectants exploit fears about not being a good parent, or a good homemaker. Those who fear they may not be liked are exploited in adverts for soaps, deodorants, spot creams and mouthwashes, and in extreme cases, cosmetic surgery. In recent times, market makers have even persuaded many of us not only to buy their merchandise, but thereby also to become mobile billboards through particular logos and motifs.

The *mass media*, now with massive technical sophistication concerning visual images, frequently manipulate by projection. Projection and association of perceptions can easily distort our visual judgments. Skilful interviewers with strong emotional needs to project a certain attitude, may, by the way they frame their questions, make the unwary say something different from what they intend. Similar techniques are used in the press, especially for headlines. Personal prejudice playing upon emotions may easily be projected into news. Channel controllers, video and desk editors are indeed powerful people in this modern era.

There is no easy way to combat the projections of others. Given an awareness of our own and others' emotional states, prejudices and biases, we are less likely to become caught up in a world of empty projection. We live in an imperfect world, and projection will always exist in many areas of life, for many unconsciously sustain, albeit often falsely, their sense of well-being though projection. Much of this we cannot change, except within our personal emotional development and that of our own close circles. These are fundamentally matters of quality child rearing and raised public awareness concerning the nature of emotional life.

Personal exercise 31

Write short notes about two examples of projection, and their consequences, within social organizations that have had particular significance for you.

10.7 Trust as social capital

Very many of our emotional reactions are determined by our sense of trust in particular environments. We have already noted that the foundations of trust, or of distrust, begin to be formed from very early in our lives. Beyond childhood and adolescence our trust in our social world requires continuous reinforcement. Even the most inwardly secure individuals, well nurtured in their youth through the experience of reliable love and commitment, are likely to have some aspects of their trust undermined by life experience. Indeed, to those who have been well nurtured and given sensitive consideration in a stable and loving family, it may be something of a shock to find that the wider world can often behave with a lack of consideration and even sometimes be indifferent to truth and justice.

Trust of course should never be blind; rather it requires discernment within each situation to test out the consistency, reliability and predictability of circumstances. Trust discards both defensive cynicism on the one hand and gullibility and foolhardiness on the other. The social world becomes grim if we are permanently on our guard, and if our first instincts are fearfully suspicious. No less, we leave ourselves open to exploitation if we appear naïve or gullible risk takers. In today's society we need to be streetwise without losing either passion or compassion.

Trust, best grown from infancy, is the most precious commodity within any society. *Trust is real social capital* starting in the cradle. *Key features* of trust are now summarized:

- Trust is essential for life and mental health, but we depend upon others for its establishment through their gifts of time, talents, tenderness, and sometimes toughness and touch.

- Trust requires faith, but not blind faith, based upon previous experience. This faith arises from patterns of the days and seasons, and from key people or things that people have made (for example bridges, ladders, and airplanes). Regularly also we require faith in ourselves, and that demands we hold ourselves in adequate self-esteem, possible only with a calm conscience.

- Trust is related to shared values, to truth and integrity; the ever-present 'faith-risk' arises from human fallibility and material imperfection.

- Words alone do not create trust. Trust requires practical action, beyond giving a promise or an undertaking, to perform and carry through service for someone else.
- Trust requires reasonable predictability and reliability in execution.
- Broken trust can be repaired, but usually neither swiftly nor easily, and demands understanding, forgiveness and forbearance amongst at least two people.

The only means by which trust can be created is through gifts of attention and mutual service. Some of these points will be helpful in the next exercise that reviews personal perceptions and experience of trusting.

Personal exercise 32

Make notes in response to the following questions:
- *Are you basically cautious or as a risk-taker? Give two examples that affirm your description, and note how these relate to your sense of trust.*
- *Recall a case when your trust was undermined, or even shattered. Outline your past and present feelings about the case, and comment upon the prospects of achievement of reparation.*

10.8 Summary of facts about feelings

Now that we have encountered some of the realities of feeling in private, small group and crowd situations, this chapter concludes with a practical summary relevant to the management of feelings:

1. Feelings exist and entwine with our personal values, views of persons, and conscience. So we need to be honest about them, that is, 'true to our feelings'.

2. In labeling our feelings, we admit them and embrace them, thus reducing the risk of projecting them inappropriately onto other people, institutions or 'systems'.

3. Some social control upon, or even repression of, certain feelings and impulses is an essential part of social and emotional wisdom. However, in the quiet of personal reflection, refraining from repression so that feelings are faced is also important for psychological and spiritual growth.

4. Where there is significant discomfort from feelings, such as guilt or persistent sadness, this signifies that there is some inner movement and repair yet to be achieved (see section 11.4 below). However, it is unlikely that troubled feelings can be fixed in an ethical vacuum, for the emotional and ethical are closely intertwined.

5. Courageous actions triggered by our feelings are sometimes called for, despite both a sense of hesitation and a sense of vulnerability. Acts do not necessarily lose their worth when inspired by emotion, even when that may not have been properly processed by the brain's cortex, as in cases of spontaneous generosity and compassion.

6. Our innate potential for receiving love, once deeply experienced and felt as generally reliable, and hence trusted, changes and transforms emotional life. The emotional learning experienced through unasked for gifts of love from others enables the transmission of new love, receivers modeling and crafting fresh capacities as givers of love.

While the potential for joy is as we have seen a basic, innate emotion, happiness and contentment are not 'givens' in life, and we sometimes have to build contentment by taking chances. The next chapter begins by examining the desire and quest for happiness and personal settlement, before moving on to consider pathways by which wounds to the human spirit may be transcended, and grief healed.

11
CONCERNING
CONTENTMENT AND
GRACING GRIEF

11
CONCERNING CONTENTMENT AND GRACING GRIEF

We have no more right to consume happiness without producing it than to consume wealth without producing it.
George Bernard Shaw, *Candida*, 1898

In solitude what happiness? Who can enjoy alone, or all enjoying, what contentment find?
Milton, *Paradise Lost*, 1667

'He is ... a man of sorrows and acquainted with grief.'
Isaiah 53:3

'My habitual pessimism is no truer than optimism, only more uncomfortable, ... and finally life-denying.'
Tim Lott, *The Scent of Dried Roses*, 1996

'He jests at scars, that never felt a wound.' ...
'What wound did ever heal but by degrees?'
William Shakespeare, 1564-1616, *Romeo and Juliet* and *Othello*

Much of the literature of human psychology has been focused upon emotional disorders, particularly negative mental states, such as depression. Over recent years more attention has been given towards 'positive' psychology through studies of happiness. This chapter concerns matters of happiness and contentment, and pathways for the resolution of aspects of grief and depression that we associate with being unhappy.

11.1 What is happiness?

Happiness can naturally be associated with the innate emotion of joy, or of the impact of pleasurable or exciting events, such as going to a good concert, a racing event or enjoying mutuality of sexual expression. But these words have a more fleeting tenor than do the terms 'inner contentment', or 'engaged with life's rich tapestry', words suggesting a more constant, creative and positive state of mind and being. This poetic stanza by Alexander Pope summarizes the dilemma of terminology concerning what we sense over 'happiness'.

> *Oh happiness! Our being's end and aim!*
> *Good, pleasure, ease, content, whatever thy name;*
> *That soothing still which prompts the eternal sigh*
> *For which to live, or dare to die.*
> From *An Essay on Man*, Epistle 4, 1734

An active inner contentment does not imply the end of a journey, or that one aspires for nothing else, or that one is complacent, let alone, fully satisfied. Contentment is no soporific or half-asleep state; rather it is a never-taken-for-granted daily outcome of serious participation in life, touching and being touched by life, engaged with life in its ever-passing moments. Contentment is achieved only 'one day at a time' through a state of hopeful aliveness of receiving sufficient 'daily bread', and in far more than the gastronomic sense, as the *Pater Noster*, the Lord's Prayer, so well summarizes.

The findings of happiness research are unsurprising. For example, the following factors tend to have *no significant lasting contribution to contentment*:

- Educational attainment (though people are happy in the short-term when passing exams).
- Conventional 'intelligence', such as high scores on IQ tests.
- Age: the young being in general no more content than the elderly.
- Money, beyond that required for basic needs. Indeed, the longing for more money and goods, and an inability to distinguish 'more' from 'enough', causes needless personal anxiety and tension for individuals and groups.

Hence, the acquisition of luxury items such as expensive motor vehicles, fine clothes, or other consumer durables, does not enhance happiness, though they may enhance physical comfort or a sense of external status.

Retail therapy, the pleasurable satisfactions of shopping, are undoubtedly short-lived. This is reflected in the fact that there has been no increase in gross levels of 'life satisfaction' amongst North Americans and Western Europeans over the past fifty years despite a doubling of inflation-adjusted income per person. We have pursued material economic development, often with ruthless efficiency from a short-term perspective, only to find ourselves with a range of social dysfunctions, such as high crime rates, obesity, increasing mental disorders, drug abuse, youth suicide, and too few reliable family and community networks. Without changes in cultural values in favor of ingredients that *do* prompt life satisfaction, these dysfunctions look destined to become all too rapidly global features.

In contrast, the pleasures of attachment to and exchange with family and friends, of being part of an active faith community, and of having regularly pleasurable hobbies, reflecting an engagement with life, are contentment enhancing. They also help people to deal with stressful life events such as loss of a loved one, or of a job or career, or moving house.

The most fundamental finding of positive psychology is that our connections with others, and with worthwhile activities that are not simply selfish, enhance personal happiness. To be, or to feel alone, with nothing special to do is the worst-case scenario for happiness. So although passing pleasures, and memorable moments, can be very important to us, they are a small part of an essentially active engagement with life; an engagement that reaches out to touch and be touched, and very different from an unreflective busyness and acquisitiveness.

Our main energies to achieve contentment are indirect, and best developed through serious engagement with friends, family, worthwhile work, hobbies and community. It is through these activities that we gain a sense of hope, of purpose, and of meaning from devotion to larger ends than ourselves. Quite simply, as emphasized in chapter 2, we are relational beings; nobodies if we have no commitments to and from other people.

So into adulthood, what do we really seek? Surely it is to make the very most of our lives, within their unavoidable and specific limitations, and to engage with real rather than false presences. Our basic nature needs were laid out in section 2.2; matters of hunger and longing were covered in section 5.3. As babies we secretly sought social encounter, engagement, and touch; physical touch and warmth of course, but, far more than that, we implicitly hoped that our lives would be touched with meaning and significance. At that fundamental level, nothing changes in our inner longings, even when we are met with vacancy, inattention and disappointment. For far too many people, such ongoing longings can be severe, prompting depression and, at worst, a wish to give up totally on life. When we become the centre of anyone's attention, even momentarily recognized, that very attention from another's presence centers us, reaffirms us as somebody special, rather than what may otherwise feel like as being of no significance. In modern jargon, focused attention gives us 'positive feed-back', the touch of an aspect of our 'daily bread'. *Mutuality through mutual attention is our fundamental condition, which if ignored will be at the massive cost of a loss of hope.*

For our lives to be touched is our constant need. We cannot live without being touched physically, emotionally, spiritually, and intellectually. Even the hermit monk in his cell is touched by Nature seen beyond his door, and by the books he reads; he is in daily contact with the people who wrote Holy Texts, and all the other books that fill his shelf, and through his faith he believes he is touched daily by the friendship of Divinity, otherwise he could not stay sane. This also is the witness of those who have survived long solitary confinement.

Human hope is kept alive by daily touch with Nature's vast storehouse. This includes plants, the seasons, birds and pets, alongside simple human contact, even through something as mundane as a 'thank you' from someone for whom we held open a door. Or it could be a smile or kind glance directed at us from a stranger. These are the 'touches' of reciprocity that help to make life worth living. So our hope resides in an expectancy of being touched on a daily basis. This is no dead-end kind of contentment. Nor is it anything like the Eastern calm acceptance of everything, where all may be 'Maya', including gruesome suffering.

11.2 Guidelines to happiness

While there is some truth in the view that we cannot simply manufacture deep happiness or contentment, any more than a physical quality such as height or shape, some relatively simple *practical guidelines to aid happiness* arise from recent research findings. Unsurprisingly, this form of advice reflects much ancient wisdom that has been long enshrined in various worldwide religious precepts, here summarized as seven statements, for everyday living:

1. *Count your blessings, and truly savor your joys.* One method of doing this is to develop the practice of a 'Joy and gratitude record' (see Practice exercise 33).

2. *Make specific acts to convey gratitude to those who have helped you.* For example, thank a mentor, or someone who had a particular and beneficial impact upon your life, more than

you realized earlier, maybe a teacher, sports coach, relative or neighbor.

3. *Become more conscious of specific acts of kindness needed to help oil a happier world.* To be conscious of planning acts of consideration and altruism is neither likely to prompt conceit about doing good, nor inhibit spontaneous generosity.

4. *Invest time in and work at your relationships.* Keep key people in mind, and let them know that you do; listen to their concerns, and also share your own. Avoid being gripped by negative ruminations about other people through cultivating a forgiving disposition that is not dependent upon apologies.

5. *Take care of your body* and its general health, for that is the present container of your spirit essence. This requires the relaxed monitoring of both diet and time use. Reflective meditation, for example, diminishes perceived stress and staves off mental disturbance.

6. *Review and renew your core commitments once a week* to remind you of your dominant values and ruling loves in life. Our 'ruling loves' are most of who and what we are.

7. *Avoid chasing money and materialism at the expense of meaning.*

Personal exercise 33

Allocate a blank notebook for recording, initially on a daily basis, the following three categories of positive data on your life. Do this regardless of mood, not ignoring things that may seem very mundane or taken too much for granted. List:

- *the things that went well for you today*
- *the joys you sensed today.*
- *the blessings you recognized today.*

Any repetition of entries from day-to-day does not matter; those will simply reinforce your sense of life. If after some time of doing this exercise, you feel in need of more positive data, then it is suggested that you review items 2 to 7 in the list above. Later maybe it will feel more appropriate to change to a weekly or monthly review.

After about 2–4 weeks of engaging in this exercise, you might find it instructive to write notes on the old adage that 'The best things in life come free'.

Note that an exercise of this kind is not essentially one of self-preoccupation. Rather it prompts a greater sense of living, aiding our demeanor to benefit both others and ourselves.

11.3 Human wounds, sadness and depression

Human beings are delicate and sensitively balanced, yet also resilient. Factors affecting our resilience include our genetic make-up, and the balance of our experience of attachment and nurture in terms of the cycles of affirmation and deprivation laid out in diagrams 9 and 10 within sections 7.6 and 7.7, pages 148 and 150. Unsurprisingly, resilience in children is mostly associated with someone being regularly available who loves them unconditionally; having an older person in or beyond the home setting with whom they can share their problems and feelings; knowing that they can make a difference to the way that things turn out, and having a sense of humor. With adults the same tends to apply, echoing section 2.2.

The nature of sadness as an innate emotion, outlined in section 5.3.3, is associated with depressed states, which are severe forms of sadness. Many depressed feelings arise from wounds to the inner spirit due to some unfulfilled need or desire for nurture, and so a sense of vacancy or loss. The feeling of being cut off at any key stage of development from crucial nurturing supplies, prompts grief and probably anger, whether displayed or hidden. Depression always diminishes life 'performance'. Here it is not appropriate to go into medical-psychiatric detail of the various forms of depression that appear in clinical cases, nor of the range of treatments on offer. We have noted that depression, though present for some in severe and pathological forms, is not basically a conventional sickness, but a part of the normal human condition. The world is an arena of both hard knocks and delights, and can never be expected to supply any of us with perfect support and affirmation when we need it, and my own view is that most of us at some stage encounter a struggle with an 'inner night'.

There are two broad classes of depression. The first, termed 'endogenous', related to distinct chemical imbalances in the bloodstream that can be managed by a range of drug therapies. The second, and more prevalent form, is 'reactive depression', and arises from external triggers that may well remind the brain, perhaps inaccurately, of earlier situations of insecurity, loneliness and threat. Reactive depression, through its mainly electrical mechanisms, may literally strike as fast as light. For some, reactive depression is associated with compulsive disorders, such as obsessions over cleanliness or household security, some of which certainly need clinical therapy. In contrast to the endogenous (biochemical imbalance) forms of depression, reactive depression seems to hook up with negative, cumulatively repressed forms of anger directed towards the self, or projected onto others or even life itself. Lack of physical exercise can accompany this and increase the sense of lonely isolation.

Depression informs us sharply of a fallen world, and of psychic and spiritual wounds, some perhaps long-repressed, not yet sufficiently identified, let alone faced out. Perversely, the wounded spirit may descend into 'pits of despair'. The triggers, never remotely intended by friends or carers, get grotesquely absorbed into the unconscious memory to create shadow material in the feeling memory. This later resonates with new happenings that trick, like a trip-wire, some perverse brain cell connections. Whatever the patterns of causality of such 'soul wounds', these can be difficult for even highly skilled helpers to uncover. Sustained but not overbearing assistance through the pits, patience and imaginative courage seem to be conditions for their healing.

Perhaps 'pit stops' in our human lives, ghastly though they can be, are essential to the soul's reparation. Many people 'motor on' with balding tires and declining inner spirits, but sooner or later depression catches up. The pit is evidence of a malady of soul, a kind of perverse megaphone calling us to pay deeper attention to ourselves, including aspects of what is present in the subconscious. All shapes of pit, whether steep-edged or of more gradual inclination, embody psychic pain which needs healing, sometimes helped by drugs, but always through the insightful commitment of at least one other person, and much courage of 'owning-up' and of taking responsibility by the sufferer.

For it is very hard for pits to be faced and truly owned; so much easier to project the blame for the 'deep blues' onto others. In facing these matters the sufferer may fear perhaps further rejection, or naïve or invalid psychiatric classification, or both. Lurid views of the eternal consequences of wrongdoing and of a general unworthiness, meted out in versions of the over-emphasized and largely pernicious doctrine of original sin, may also contribute to depressive tendencies.

Critical or 'snap out of it' talk, so understandable as reactions from bystanders, is the last thing that a depressive sufferer needs in their states of distasteful unsociability, and self-other hate, that may oscillate along a wide spectrum of feelings and actions:

LOW END   Suicidal…Desolation…Stability/Consolation…

    …Hyperactivity… **Manic actions   HIGH END**

Drugs prescribed in this context aim to medicate mood. Antidepressants stimulate artificially to alter brain states at the low end to raise pleasure; tranquillizers and sedatives address the high end to moderate excessive elation.

In desolation the sufferer needs to hold onto a thread of faith that its ghastliness will pass; in consolation to make the most of the calm; and in hyperactive 'highs' to be alert and wary of a possible hurtling swing towards another precipice. Most of these matters are a tussle with 'the inward parts', but paradoxically, there is no dark shadow without also light. So hope's renewal may be just around the corner, as sometimes, when all energy has been extinguished, some mystical 'hand' reaches down into the pit, and grace appears. This is, partly at least, a matter of spiritual movement, a grace indeed, not essentially dependent upon drug therapy.

11.4 Personal solvency and pathways of gracing grief

Quality of life involves our inner essence. We need to spark adequately and to remain solvent without excessive striving. This requires an absence of deep fearfulness or panic, and to be realistically buttressed from excess negativity and the worst fallouts from depressive tendencies. The upper half of diagram 12 is a summary of the pathways through which the human emotional spirit may become damaged. This diagram has universal implications and applications, for nobody in this life escapes some grief. The lower half of the diagram shows pathways of repair, or otherwise.

Diagram 12: Pathways of Grief and Growth

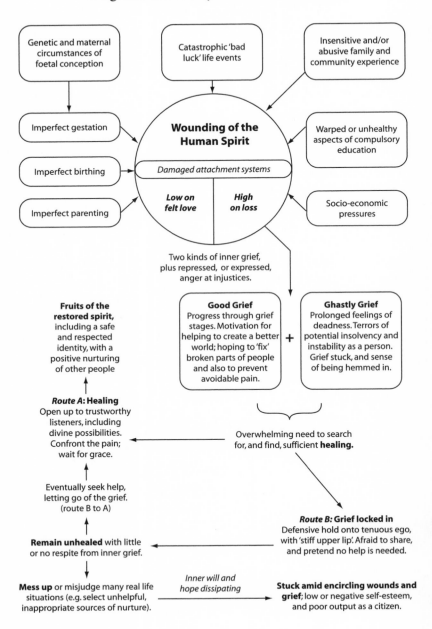

Within the connections of diagram 12, two pathways of resolution (A and B, the latter less direct) are encountered. It is through these pathways that 'wounds of the spirit', in their variety, may be healed, or (at the bottom right of the diagram) may continue to perpetuate within a descending cycle of emotional deprivation as portrayed earlier in diagram 10, page 150. Somehow, grief has to be 'graced' to be healed of its worst and often perpetuating impacts.

Wounds of the spirit may include premature loss of a parent, or spouse or lover from a variety of causes, including illness or accident; feeling loved only through good behavior or achievement; or a major family or career disappointment. These examples may be gathered within the broad category of 'bad luck life events' shown at the top of diagram 12.

Sharing pains of loss with an accepting and focused listener is a frequently therapeutic route, and the basis for much skilled counseling as well as close friendship. Drugs do not directly grace grief, though they can contain its initially acute and perhaps depressive impacts on a temporary basis while a larger rebalancing of the inner spirit takes place over time. When external anxiety or internal insecurity shake and threaten our spirit's equilibrium and solvency, our urge, if not our confidence, is to communicate, to dialogue in spirit and in truth, so as to escape defensive isolation and despair.

Personal exercise 34

Reflect unhurriedly upon diagram 12 before naming two wounds from which you believe that your spirit suffers, whether in time past or in the present. Estimate their year-date origins, and then complete a table in your notebook as follows.

Spirit wounds and associated factors	Example 1 (dating from.............)	Example 2 (dating from ....)
Wound described with its associated feelings.		
Believed origin or cause(s) of the wound.		
Present manifestations in personal behavior.		
Avenues of healing experienced so far.		
Sense of the future in relation to the wound.		

On the basis of your examples, frame a single consequential personal resolve. This might be, for example, to discuss the table with a trusted friend or partner.

11.5 Associated questions of human existence

Our emotions are clearly far from being merely complex 'brain events' and are related to a great variety of factors in our lives. Included amongst these are our perceptions and views upon the large questions of human existence and purpose that have troubled the human heart and mind ever since recorded history began.

Beyond basic biological survival, human motivation is impelled by often unspoken searches for meaning. This searching is emotionally loaded, and dependent upon experience in a range of social settings. While we may retreat from the world and into the silence of our individuality, it has been emphasized in this text that we depend from birth upon social relationships, and their direct and indirect teaching, for a sense of personal identity and hope.

Within our unique capacity for reflection, is the meandering of our minds amongst key interlinked *existential questions*, here listed sequentially.

1. *Who am I?* This is the question of identity, most helpfully linked to an evolving 'personal story' of our life that in its telling makes sense to us.

2. *How am I made and how do I tick?* This is the question of understanding the relationships between the parts of body, mind, emotion and character and how they function.

3. *How did I, and others, get here?* This is the question of our physical and cultural origins.

4. *Where do I belong?* This is the question of personal roots, and key spatial relationships.

5. *Would I be missed, and if so by whom?* This is the question of key human attachments.

6. *Are there any covenant promises?* This is the question concerning the ethics of relational commitment and the hope derived through its practice.

7. *What is the point of life, particularly of my life, in its sequence in time?* This is the question of personal meaning.

8. *What are the risks to developing an authentic life?* This question includes possible economic or psychological insolvency, and of the possibility of living a lie to one's inner essence, what can be called possible 'snakebites' in the shadow lands of the soul.

9. *What is my destiny?* This is the question of my aims and ambitions now, of my eventual hopes for my earthly legacy, and possibly also of some 'ladder' to a heavenly eternity.

10. *So who am I?* This is the same question as the first in the list, and includes what I aspire to be and become in this world, as both separate and connected, amid the ever shrinking moments of my Earth time.

All these fundamental questions depend upon the uniquely human trait of *reflective capability* that a balanced education worthy of the name should aim to develop in a range of fields for all students according to their stage of development. The question sequence has an internal circular logic since 1 and 10 are essentially the same, separated by one full cycle of holistic reflection. There are of course no final answers to these questions in this life. We are not static exhibits, but dynamic evolving and interacting beings seeking to construct a decent life rather than an existence, while finding a sufficient ease and contentment in the process.

Sadly, mainstream educational priorities tend to prompt us to study almost everything about the world except the nature and purposes of ourselves as persons. It is therefore unsurprising that our besetting problems are mostly personal and inter-personal, with a high emotional content, rather than technological. Understanding how we tick as individuals and in relationships is not inherently the specialist business of counseling psychologists, therapists and psychiatrists. Insights into mood and meaning are an essential part of being and becoming human. They involve several forms of 'literacy'; capabilities and skills very different from those obsessively assessed in formal educational provision, notably in spheres of emotional, ethical and spiritual life.

Personal exercise 35

Study the sequence of ten questions shown above. After reflection, including some review of diagram 12 above, and your response to that in exercise 34, note the two or three questions that most interest or trouble you at the moment, and outline why. This is likely to suggest important agenda for your future growth as a person living ever more comfortably, though not complacently, 'in your own skin'.

11.6 Shaping life stories

An adequate view of human identity has to accommodate more than our genes, gender, social roles, lifestyles, ambitions and actions. We are only our past, and our present at the 'this moment'. Futures are yet to be experienced, shaped and negotiated. It is a small step from envisaging human *identity as 'life story'*, a reflective account of ourselves that we can 'tell', and re-tell, to ourselves and trusted others, to recognizing that our personal story is also an unfolding 'document', a personal 'gospel', the gospel according to you and to me. I believe that such life 'stories', like life itself, embody sacred qualities.

As we try to understand ourselves, and the sometimes scattered fragments and muddied waters of our lives with all manner of emotional material, we create 'text' of both words and images. Some dare to publish their autobiographies, linking fragments, generally chronologically, though the late playwright Arthur Miller's *Timebends* is a fascinating exception. A few, even more daringly, leave us accounts of their spiritual journeys (see, for example, those of 'Loran Hurnscot' and Philip Toynbee in the select bibliography). Such documents inevitably have many missing fragments, whether from memory loss (accidental or repressed), or tact and consideration for others, or from a conscious lack of desire or courage to dig out and face the whole 'true' story. Pastoral care work, in its widest sense, from good neighboring to psychiatry, involves being an agent to help others pick up the fragments of and to sustain their story. These fragments are sometimes frighteningly dispersed and jumbled up by mental disturbance, loneliness and lack of roots.

Every Christmastide embodies a fundamental call to identify with the wonder and vulnerability of babies, which is where new 'gospel stories' begin. We are yet to secure in consequence a fresh cultural admiration for mothers and fathers in their crucial parenting vocations upon which literally everything future hangs. We cannot create markedly better societies without such commonsense and research-informed practical and emotional investment. We forget that today's babies are the inheritors of a century of man-made holocausts that, as history, dwarf prior events. If we could grasp that reality we would work tirelessly to create the foundations of love stories that eradicate the sad facts of psychological and spiritual genocide for so many of today's babies and infants. While later rescue is possible, it is generally much more complex, and, inevitably, vastly more expensive.

Some of the scars of emotionally bleak childhood probably never vanish completely. *The most serious structural sin of our historic inheritance is that we do not treasure babies and those who bear them.* Thus, so irrationally, such neglect guarantees that most of our well-intentioned efforts at social and educational improvement have much diminished impacts. The greatest contentment for the greatest number is sadly a goal now rarely debated, let alone addressed by political parties and implemented by governments.

Having recognized the associations of feelings and emotions with human spirituality, our journey here now takes us on to a more detailed examination of the spiritual sixth sense

12
FEELING DIVINE: SPIRITUAL DEVELOPMENT AND HUMAN STORY

12
FEELING DIVINE:
SPIRITUAL DEVELOPMENT
AND HUMAN STORY

'We are not human beings on a spiritual journey. Rather we are
spiritual beings on a human journey.'
Teilard de Chardin; 1881-1955

'Psychiatry has not only neglected but actively ignored
the issue of spirituality.'
M Scott Peck

'My emotions flowered in me like a divine revelation.'
Andre Gide, 1869-1951, in *The Fruits of the Earth*

'Seeing is believing, but feeling is God's own truth.'
Irish proverb

'The true meaning of religion is morality touched by emotion.'
Matthew Arnold, 1822-88, in *Literature and Dogma*

It was noted in section 9.5 that 'spiritual disciplines' can assist us in
emotional management. Emotional language and experience
intermingle with the 'spiritual realm', whether a theological frame of
reference is specific, non-existent, or not identified. This chapter opens
out some analysis of our spiritual 'sixth sense'.

12.1 What is the spiritual?

There are no easy intellectual definitions of the human spiritual dimension, but that does not detract from its reality that can become more tangible if we consider its nature from a range of angles. We can view the spiritual as that which transcends or rises above and beyond all else that we experience, yet connected by mysterious threads to our everyday experience when pondered and held in contemplation. Involved is an awareness of a 'presence' greater than the self and other human beings that embodies a sharpening of connectional truth. Highlighted by research on the spiritual development of children, David Hay suggests that an active spirituality endows us with an enhanced relational consciousness.

Unsurprisingly, the spiritual often contains moral and theological components. It is implicitly interwoven with emotional life, and sometimes related to an aesthetic or artistic context provided perhaps by music, poetry, landscape and architecture. This poem expresses something of this natural spiritual dimension, plumbed into our biological potential as a 'sixth sense' of humankind.

Spiritual Flow

There is an energy that physics does not measure;
The mystic mind terms this 'spiritual treasure'.
Such energy flows through surprise constellations,
When 'be' attitudes' eyes open fresh permutations;
And the world is viewed as an awesome creation,
Beyond neat prescription, even complex equation,
As contemplatives search for ultimate meanings,
Using fine arts' love-stories during their screenings.
Within this delicate, silk-spun spiritual tent
Disparate chains link as surprise and extent;
New soul-friends emerge, in unsought affirmation
For holding faith in mythical form is sanity's station.

From *Purpose in Presence,* page 31

There is a serious literature of spirituality, both ancient and modern, though in modern culture few of us are encouraged to become spiritually literate, and this in part undermines our capacities for emotional management. Although much that is spiritual is tacitly repressed in adult conversation, one fairly recent serious survey suggested that about two-thirds of adults in contemporary society acknowledge spiritual experience as an aspect of their reality. Despite such prevalence of spiritual experiences, in our culture we remain embarrassed to talk about them beyond childhood. Even young children by the time they reach the mid-primary years realize that spiritual imagination tends not to be a natural part of 'grown-up' talk. A great deal is lost through such adult repression and embarrassment about an aspect of our total being.

I have had a few distinct and memorable spiritual experiences that counterbalance some sudden, though thankfully short reactive depressions. Such happenings are hard to define because they are totally unplanned and have mysterious, unpredictable qualities. In my case they have been associated with what, in retrospect, seem relatively simple recognitions of non-judgmental truth and connection. Experienced in a context of seriousness, such moments have both aided my resilience, and endowed me with memories of an inner buoyancy and lightness, grounding my sense of hope despite our lack of consistent focus upon issues that are rationally of most importance.

True being is at the heart of spirituality, and the characteristics of a spiritual experience are essentially ecstatic (from the Greek *ekstasis*) in which, momentarily, we seem to stand outside ourselves, while at the same time remaining rooted, yet uplifted and transformed from within. There is some evidence that such transcendent experience may be activated through the brain's temporal lobes (see diagram 3, page 60) but this is far from suggesting that a soul-centre is located in a particular part of the brain!

12.2 Spiritual intelligence enhances relational consciousness

Chapter 2 emphasized the relational nature of human reality, what amounts to a continual 'dance' between the inner and outer aspects of life, and between 'self' and 'other'. Chapter 3 suggested that our biological systems are of awe-inspiring complexity. So we can perceive that the relational world, orchestrated and resonating within our heads and hearts, each with a unique and delicate history, is more marvelous than we can possibly contemplate, and only poorly accessible to consciousness (as noted in section 10.3).

Research on the spirituality and worldviews of young children now suggests that spirituality is biologically and psychologically natural to us, akin to what I have called our 'sixth sense'. Hence the spiritual dimension is implicit. However, particularly as we are deemed to 'grow up', we can and do ignore this substratum, choosing to live entirely or predominantly materially and 'concretely', marginalizing the spiritual imagination whose existence presents no problems of principle for many distinguished scientists and artists.

A further extension of the concept of 'intelligence', beyond the relational and emotional encountered in section 2.3 is the possibility of *spiritual intelligence*. Such 'intelligence' pervading spiritual development seems to be associated with four interconnected broad features:

- It is open to diversity, and muses upon fundamental questions of life purpose as outlined in section 11.5.
- It has the capacity to face and use adversity and suffering, promoting inner growth of the personality through struggle, sometimes ethical struggle.
- It quarries everyday situations, namely 'ordinary' experience, whether comfortable or uncomfortable, uplifting or distressing, so as to extend and enhance interpretations and perceptions of the totality of environment.
- It creates conditions for an enhanced relational consciousness, supporting people with patient grace during periods of trial, and illuminating them in times of joy.

Some thirty years ago, the late Sir Alister Hardy, in his retirement from an Oxford professorship in Biological Sciences, began to compile what is now an extensive archive of spiritual experiences. In these, people frequently report that their spiritual experience prompts them to take a more holistic perspective on life, with an increased desire to care for others, to work for social justice and for greater respect of the biophysical environment. Such convictions are often accompanied by a reduced preoccupation with materialism, and shifts in life purpose or vocation. Received privately as specific touches upon the soul-centre, these experiences tend to endow an equanimity and contentment amid fresh challenges concerning how lifetime is spent. Hence, spiritual life is health-promoting as emotions disruptive of the soul-centre become attenuated and then transfigured.

Though innate in every person, the spiritual is like a tender garden plant that can easily be choked or squeezed out without active cultivation. Even ostensibly charitable activities, 'worthy causes', can inhibit spiritual development. This is a common testimony amongst the many varieties of 'full-time religious'. In their vocations they must guard against becoming entrapped amid the strain of others' needs and an unremitting drive for or expectancy to do 'good works'. All of us, regardless of our station in life, 'profit little if we gain the whole world and lose our own soul-centre', or fail to be 'true to our own inner self', to paraphrase the wisdom of Jesus and Shakespeare.

So how shall we envision and describe the nature of the human soul appropriately for our times? What lies at the very centre of being a person, and can be touched by grace?

12.3 Envisioning the soul

Amongst many of my contemporaries as a youngster, I acquired a view of the soul as a tiny part within each human being, yet to be tracked down anatomically. This soul was some small presence near to the heart, or perhaps the near the front the head, behind the temple. It was a kind of inner secret centre that someday maybe I would discover, though for the time being only God knew about it or could see it. Perhaps this tiny soul was indeed God's image, shrunk infinitesimally and planted safely, but secretly, in each person.

Those perceptions are actually far from being superficial, though over the matter of 'size' I am no longer comfortable. Now I perceive the soul as large rather than tiny. As I see it, all our senses, thoughts, feelings and emotions, virtues and bodily presence are incorporated into 'soul' as a multidimensional reality through the bending forms of time past, present, future and into eternity. In fact I would go as far as to say that our whole is our soul. I have developed my own model for this, and explain this in diagram 13 below.

Diagram 13: Representation of the human soul

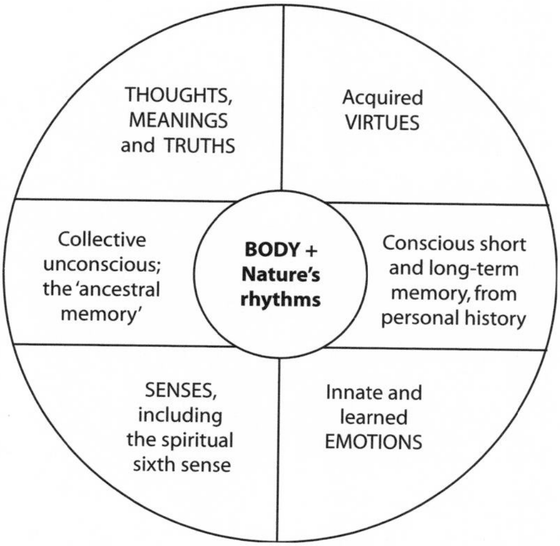

This picture of the soul is one of wholeness, a circular enfoldedness. Included are all the key areas of sensing, thinking, emoting, and behaving that combine as and contribute to human personality. Our physical bodies at the centre, forever changing, renewing and decaying in our earthly life, are set within Creation's rhythms of night and day; the tides and the cycles of the Moon, and the four seasons of blossom, growth and harvest, decay and dormancy. Noted also are the interfaces of both conscious personal history, and the unconscious. The latter includes what can be termed our 'ancestral memory', or what Carl Jung termed 'the collective unconscious'.

Though I have no wish to make unreal distinctions between 'the secular' and 'the sacred', I emphasize that this kind of model does not require allegiance to any particular religious propositions or doctrines. From a religious perspective the model can be seen as interfaces through which God's image expresses itself through each unique human personality. From a Christian viewpoint, all that needs to be said here is that the Jesus of history was a real part of our human world, come to planet Earth like one of us. He lived a consciously godly life, sharing in the everyday through joinery, fishing, feeding, chatting, teaching, debating, disappointment, forgiveness, temptation, tears, and so on, but displayed unconditional love of a clearly amazing depth. Rejected by his own people, who looked for something far more majestic, Jesus taught *basic principles of universal laws of love* by whose energy he lived, transcending a death delivered by love's antithesis, thereby extending the physical world directly into the spiritual.

12.4 Conditions for spiritual growth

While it is not essential to have a particular religious faith to have spiritual experience, people who have spiritual experiences are it seems often led towards religious faith. Religion is a very important way of making sense of spiritual experience and integrating it into the whole of life. Without religious faith, spiritual experience tends to lead nowhere, or become destructive by leading to a vague spiritualism or even occultism. Yet religion attached more to legalism than to love can be intensely divisive and unattractive, providing much unhelpful baggage even for good people to bear.

All the stages of the life-course are relevant to the growth of spirituality, a 'sense' that is in principle never dormant. Parents may encourage and enhance natural spiritual awareness in their children, but they need to be spiritually mature themselves and to give time to developing good relationships with their children. When these two are present, spiritual development just happens, for close relationships have a dynamic integrity through which spirituality can operate.

The *permitting conditions* for spiritual development, though they have no single logical order, may be summarized as follows.

- A shift in personal values, often prompted by unease with the ways in which present personal time, energy and money are being consumed. This in essence incorporates a review of what it means to live ethically, and in truth, as a freed spirit, partly through new encounters with the great, timeless, and culturally unspecific virtues, particularly *honesty* (with humility), *justice* (seeking for others what is their due), *compassion* (selfless love), *discernment* (prudence), *fortitude* (courage displayed amid altruism) and *moderation* (temperance). The renewal of our values reorients motivation, awakens the deep soul's desires and reduces our attention towards what amounts to habits and cravings that are not ultimately crucial for our well-being.

- A calming of the intellectual mind, calling upon the life of the ethical imagination, and allowing spiritual vision some space, an opportunity for visitation. This may include considerations of psychological healing (see diagram 12, page 226) alongside a desire to manage unstable feelings towards greater consistency of living by love.

- Opening all windows of human 'intelligence' in the spirit, developing a perceptive, multicolored understanding of and wisdom about life. Expressing the spirit in actions, embracing generosity, giving opportunity for compassion and for a 'beyond duty' joy of the call to be of service.

- Cultivating a commitment to the arts of contemplative reflection and prayer, perhaps with some participation in congenial quality worship. Retreats and various courses that aim to develop spiritual self-awareness may help, as can meditation upon works of art or getting in touch with the beauty, fascination and variety of nature. Through reflection we create the conditions for sensing 'a Real Presence'. Some call this 'waiting upon God', a kind of prayer without words in which listening is far more necessary than speaking, though we may find some visual imagery, or gentle music, helpful as channels to focus this ever-available if not immediately felt gift of grace.

All such development is aided if we recognize that our condition so often in modern culture is that of 'displaced persons'. We often live in dislocation from our incarnate core, the essence of our spiritual home. So, like refugees, we have to learn how to make a home, roots, and sufficient identity in a different 'country' (whatever our fears and feelings), or simply die or live by lie in one way or another. Now we may be well reminded of the root meaning of the word 'religion', being to re-relate, re-balance and re-join, so putting back together and healing the wounds of fragmentation of self and of separation between self and others.

Personal exercise 36

Imagine two countries, one of vice and one of virtue. Vice-land is governed by a One Party State based upon the vices listed. Virtue-land is governed by a democratically elected Parliament in which all parties hold to the directly contrasting virtues listed.

Vice-land	Virtue-land
Dishonesty	Honesty
Injustice	Justice
Indifference	Compassion
Arrogance about ignorance	Wisdom and discernment
Fear and foolhardiness	Courageous altruism
Hunger or extravagance	Moderation and temperance

Write journal notes about what it would be like to live in Vice-land and in Virtue-land.

12.5 The relational imperative of divine feeling

We need each other both in order to be and to become what Jung termed 'individuated'. This is our unavoidable ethical reality. For this reason no society has evolved, let alone survived, without shared understandings about rites of passage and publicly witnessed promises, particularly between men and women for procreation and childrearing.

We have noted that without secure love, souls become lost, lonely, isolated, and at risk of a range of pathologies. We need all the loving security we can get, especially in our early growth to prompt deep emotional confidence about learning, and to help sustain a wide range of capabilities for a lifetime, thereby preventing burnout or depression and desolation in the challenging tight corners of life. One recent voice of truth, Martin Luther King, five years before his tragic murder, wrote:

'The means by which we live have outdistanced the ends for which we live. Our scientific power has outrun our spiritual power. We have guided missiles and unguided men.'

From *Strength to Love*, 1963

By all means possible we need to establish a stability of identity in both vertical and horizontal dimensions. Diagram 14 is one attempt to picture aspects of this, showing key disciplines and fields of understanding within both a rooted vertical 'upright posture' and a horizontal 'arms open' inter-dependence.

Diagram 14: Becoming secure within both horizontal and vertical dimensions

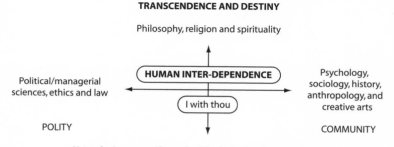

12.6 Consequences of spiritual capability

In summary, spirituality promotes the finding and reconnecting of the total authentic self within the diversity and complexity of the Universe. This potential is not an optional extra for the pious or creedal religious, but a crucial driver of motivation, hope, an integrated identity and of a life filled with zest and meaning. Furthermore, the spiritual dimension enables a comfortable-enough living with paradox and assuages loss and grief that, along with attachment and love, are fundamental to the human condition.

We have noted that spirituality may be cultivated through many areas of experience and daily life, provided we find real space for getting in touch with our deepest personal thoughts and feelings at the root of our being. It thus requires pause and quiet, so we can tap into its power and practical potential from the discipline of reflection. This demands that we suspend 'living by reaction', and to re-learn to 'live inside-out', which paradoxically is what we all did quite naturally as infants.

Spiritual insight arrives by receptivity rather than through talking. Solutions to problems and resolutions of struggles often come with a calm simplicity when all conventional energies are spent. Receptivity to spiritual grace is more likely when our emotions are settled and not near high or low extremes. Time then seems to get suspended as a sense of safety and comfortableness emerges at the time and place of reflection.

Developing our spiritual capacity makes us both fully human and fully alive, and oils the work of mutuality and love that is our ultimate purpose of being. So the flame of hope is kept alive beyond the negative polarizations of fear and distrust. The riches of spirituality also help us to approach death with a genuine peace with ourselves and with the world. That is of no minor importance, for the approach of death is our only certainty in life in the present.

Coming to terms with the reality of both positive and negative possibilities in our practical, emotional, and moral universe, and exercising courage within both mutual and soul-self-interest, is the fundamental challenge to all of us in seeking and bequeathing a better world. This is all too awesome without recognizing and feeding the spiritual, availing ourselves of the possibilities of hopeful association with 'the first cause' that gave us breath and life.

All religion at its core is about humankind finding relationships to one higher source, a 'Creative Mastermind' perhaps, that is aware of our 'mind-fields' or 'souls', yet through respect of our individuality and preciousness choosing not to control us as if we were puppets. All the major world faiths have a perception of a God within that can fill us to make us more than the complex sum of our parts; and we have seen how immensely unfathomable is the detail of our emotional brain and its electrochemical processes.

It seems that religions are always capable of being corrupted when leaders and cliques emerge who, perhaps through poverty of emotional formation, become more pre-occupied with pronouncing their version of God's will to their people from the comfort of ecclesiastical hierarchy, than with showing them *how to find this direction and energy within themselves*, as persons respectfully 'created as Divine image'. Kenneth Cragg, sometime Anglican Bishop in Jerusalem, and having a deep understanding of religions in the Middle East, put religious integrity this way:

> 'A right theology has sterner tasks within the psyche than within the mind. "Truth in the inward parts" is more exacting than the logic of a credo, the niceties of a ritual or the benchmarks of a discipline. Realism about religion is a vital element in our discovery of each other. For our inner compromises, our private and collective sins in the practice of religion have a spiritual kinship that no honesty can mistake.'
> *Troubled by Truth*, 1992, page 269

Personal exercise 37

The tasks for this penultimate exercise are in principle simple, but could turn out to be quite demanding. More than one period of reflection about the tasks may well be needed. First, consider your nature as being more than your physical body. Diagrams 13 and 14 (page 239 and 243) may be helpful concerning this. Then make three columns on a fresh sheet of your personal notebook with the headings as follows.

My fundamental personal longings	The main ways in which each longing is presently being met	Other avenues through which the longing might be satisfied

In the left hand column, list between about three and ten examples of your deepest longings. Then alongside each longing, complete the remaining two columns.

Now comment upon whether your 'table' then leaves any significant and legitimate 'holes' or vacancies of apparently unfulfillable longings in your life. Finally write a note upon how, if at all, this exercise might change one aspect of your approach to life, including what you might do about any vacant longings.

13
EPILOGUE – SUSTAINING HOPE AND EMOTIONAL POISE

13
EPILOGUE – SUSTAINING
HOPE AND EMOTIONAL POISE

'You say you must avoid books which deal with feelings; but the mystics
don't deal with feelings, but with love, which is a very different thing. You
have too many feelings, but not nearly enough love.'
Evelyn Underhill, 1875-1941, *Letters*

'Hope grew all around me like a twisting vine,
And fruits, and foliage, not my own, seemed mine.'
Samuel Coleridge, *Dejection: An ode*, 1802

'What I dream of is an art of balance, of purity and serenity, a soothing
and calming influence on the mind, rather like a good armchair which
provides relaxation from physical fatigue.'
Henri Matisse, 1908

'I am, therefore I emote, and thus can interpret thought, predict
consequences of action, and make effective choices.'
Damasio, 1994

In this last quotation, neuroscientist Damasio takes a justified tilt at philosopher Rene Descartes' (1596-1650) famous phrase 'I think, therefore I am'. This manifestly limiting and warped view of human nature has had a huge influence upon the subsequent development of Western thought, setting up an unhelpful polarized dualism between mind and matter. It has for example contributed to some unnecessary tensions between science, spirituality and religion, and has narrowed the practice of education, now dominated by narrowed perceptions of human capability and development. Perhaps the most compelling truism is that '*I am loved, and can love, therefore I am*'.

Our origins in the womb begin very shortly after conception when the fertilized ovum attaches securely to the uterine wall of our biological mothers. Without that attachment, the secluded, secret origin of transmitted nature-nurture, the fertilized egg could not begin to grow, and we would never be, let alone become somebody. This is the implicit pattern of all life thereafter. Amazingly, by a mere four weeks after that first attachment, about half a million neurons per minute migrate within the fetus mainly, but not exclusively, towards what eventually becomes the human brain. Along with this migration and electrochemical concentration, some two million synapses form per second in this primitive tissue (see diagram 2 page 56, and also Table 7, page 75). These are truly awesome beginnings, and real miracles of life.

The delicate primal emotional aspects of early human growth processes are, as has been emphasized, subject to great influences from both their chemical and social environments. Concerning these, both the physical and psychological health of mothers is paramount. Beyond their basic layout, our brains are fundamentally sculpted for both good and ill by our experiences. In particular, inconsistent, unreliable early nurture, experienced as 'sharp-edged' and so involving unseen emotional trauma for tiny youngsters, can cause deformities in critical parts of the brain, such as the corpus callosum, so harming communication between the two hemispheres of the cortex. While such features can be compensated for later, through regular tender, loving care, and wounds healed, unhelpful brain circuits can still be switched on in emotionally threatening circumstances, something akin to scar tissue that can still be capable of coming alive to cloud our days.

13.1 Distorted perceptions and assumptions

Given the problematic and too often brutal history of Western civilization that is our ancestral inheritance, I imagine that most of us are forgiven many times over for not taking seriously enough a creative and reflective approach to our inner lives, plumbing as appropriate our shadow selves and any associated scars of hidden, un-named trauma. In our modem cultures there are many more beguiling distractions and counter-attractions than ever before. *Collectively we are at a crossroads, and we need new ethical and spiritual vision that faces our insistent longings for reliable nurture, meaning and significance.*

The majority in past ages may have ignored the inner call to emotional and spiritual growth, inseparable from psychological maturation, during their struggles for basic survival, though the archaeological evidence suggests otherwise, and that a sense of the spiritual, that we may be tempted to discount as primitive, formed the centre of many thriving cultures. Our ancestors certainly had considerable agricultural expertise without the benefit of books, let alone modern communications systems and the aggregate wisdom of the natural and social sciences. Now we have no rational excuse for marginalizing our inner nature that drives so much of our outward action. If we desire ecological survival, we now have to take seriously the expansive possibilities of our science-informed imagination. 'Many are called, but few choose to listen and act', Jesus asserted. Here the 'call' is to emotional, relational and spiritual literacy, and to make it tangible and attractive, even though selecting details of our individual pathways is ultimately a personal matter which none of us can claim by proxy.

The westernized cultural assumption of competitive achievement, requiring a singleness of purpose, is almost certainly incompatible with the biophysics and biochemistry of our evolutionary brains, with our psychological well-being, and with being a good-enough mother or father. Most of all, it is too often at odds with the wisdom of a grander mind in which non-industrialized societies placed their hope and the power of whose loss is modernity's greatest irrationality. The 'Significant Absence' could yet become a 'Real Presence' for a New Enlightenment, which education must reformulate before personal and social atomization possibly become too irreversible.

Secular materialism essentially reduces emotions to epi-phenomena, best dealt with by seeing them as essentially transient. Brain research is showing us differently, confirming our suspicions that our emotions really are a deep part of us from as early as the second trimester of fetal gestation (see again Table 7, page 75). They are here to be managed rather than put up with in their capriciousness. Hence a detachment of the cognitive-intellectual self from the emotional self is a complete blind alley. Such separation is unworthy of all of us, whatever our emotional, intellectual and motor gifts and abilities. Thoughts, events, acts and emotions are each elements in the warp and weft of our lives, or what we may call our 'composite story'; and *our story is enriched, even explained, by learning to feel intelligently.*

In seeking to give some practice in marshalling thinking about feeling, while being spiritually informed, this book has endeavored to be respectful of faith, and hopefully unthreatening to people of no particular religious conviction, though we have noted that everyone who is even remotely conscious inevitably lives by faith. What we now know from brain science, and which confirms what reflective and mystical people have known for centuries, is that *what we feel leads to how we think.* So whatever you and I think about anything, including religion, is affected by our feelings, and our feelings have a long history.

Our essence or 'soul' accommodates all matters of our substance to give us, as shown in diagram 13 (page 239), a more integrated but still mysterious model of human life and possibility. We humans are of awesome complexity, and our lives are in nature both dynamic and changing. Our human relations are essentially concerned with sharing, in varied proportions, the dynamic complexities of individuals, set in what are now, for most people, stretching and disorienting social settings. We are unlikely ever to know ourselves, let alone another person completely; hence boredom with each other, let alone our babies and infants is, in part at least, a failure of imagination. If we are significantly estranged from ourselves in all our variety, we willhave difficulties with others, being unable to behave with appropriate consideration.

13.2 Hopeful bearings

All of us need articles of faith and gifts of reliable love and friendship, but also hope as we rise from our beds each morning. Hope involves holding on to some great aspiration, a vision, a beautiful dream, or, perhaps best of all, a framework of promises endowed without our asking, what the Old Testament calls 'covenant'. 'Hoping against hope' means hanging on to some optimistic possibility for each day that John Keble sensed in the first line of his 19th-century hymn, 'New every morning is the love'. There can be no leadership without hope and vision that taps and arouses our best energies.

Hence *hope is a near aspect of our essence*, a motivator of our 'sparks', our best energies. There can be little motivation without hope. Not least, our young people need to encounter well rooted, sparkling, genuine and truly alive rather than wearied adults. Their role models and teachers must be men and women in touch with their 'inward parts', not simply resource technicians within fields of knowledge.

Reflecting upon where hope comes from Vaclav Harvel, former President of the democratic Czech Republic, a brave man formed under the repressive austerities of Soviet-dominated communism, believes that:

'The gift and virtue of hope comes from elsewhere; it transcends the world that is immediately experienced, and is anchored somewhere beyond its horizons, its deepest roots being transcendental.'

From *Living in Truth*, Faber, 1990

Hope is neither optimism, nor a mere derivative of something here, of some movement, or of some favorable sign in the world; neither is it derived simply from emotions such as innate joy. Hope is rather the certainty that something makes sense, and will go on making sense, continuing to enshrine meaning regardless of how short-term events are turning out.

The maintenance of hope is related to probabilities of continuing to live without being seriously dislocated from our cherished values. It has been emphasized that our emotions are in practice entwined with our ethics (see, for example, sections 2.5 and 4.5). A good life is in respects a series of delicate balancing acts between competing dispositions and options. This is the rich fabric of choices, now more than ever available to us both socially and scientifically, with a paradox that the wider the choice, the greater the risks of losing our way.

13.3 Living in holistic ethical balance

Aristotle's ethical system was based upon the notion that the virtues are midpoints between having too much and too little of an emotion. So, for example, the virtue of courage lies between having too much fear (that we might call 'timidity'), and too little fear (that we might call 'foolhardiness'). Implicitly this is not remote from what we now call 'emotional intelligence' (see section 2.3). That in effect involves striking a balance between emotion and reason, with neither in complete control.

A living rather than dry, doctrinal view of ethics takes in our heartfelt drives. Without moral sentiments to guide our moral reasoning we would merely tend to obey the letter of moral law than live within the spirit of the law, a matter that again can find echoes in the teaching of Jesus and others. We are called to 'live in spirit and in truth' yet dare not yet take that guideline seriously! Acts are far from losing their moral worth when inspired by emotion, when that functions to guide our moral behavior. Spontaneous kindness and generosity, for example, are intuitively far more appealing than if outgoing actions have been coldly rationalized.

This book has emphasized that innate and learned emotions are crucial to active, reflective management so that we may grow in hope and sensitivity. We have seen that emotional life is intimately interwoven with our relational capacities and potentials. Those now call for changed priorities to enable the social world to cohere and to function more effectively. No individual is an island; we can do no other than define ourselves through our relationships, and this places cycles of attachment and loss near the centre of our emotional being. Social attachment as a primary mammalian drive therefore, and unsurprisingly, acts as a powerful moderator of our emotional life, with its joys, stresses, strains, pains and gains.

Our relational journey is aided if we have been well formed emotionally and spiritually in our early years, and continue to tap into the vast history of spiritual encounter, giving our imagination space for unearthing its possibilities. *We cannot live without faith's anchor; neither without hope's allure; nor without love's possibilities.* That is where an active and contemplative religious life is often helpful, endowing existential meaning for our best endeavors, provided that we do not become encumbered with divisive over-intellectualized doctrinal propositions that feed the hierarchical baggage of much organized religion. The Carpenter of Nazareth, the most important figure in Western cultural history, and many saints since, including near our time, Ghandi, Martin Luther-King and Mother Theresa, lived in ways that warned of organized religion's potential to divide, to sap and drain soul-spirit.

13.4 Emotional mastery within community

If you have stayed with the bulk of this text's presentation, for no book is a perfect communication, you will hopefully be more emotionally literate than you were, and perhaps feel encouraged in the quest for emotional, and indeed spiritual mastery, a much gentler and more possible goal than some abstract perfection. Whether you are now measurably improving as a practical 'manager' of your own varied 'up and down' emotional life is likely to be a longer process than one reflective read of a book like this, though the personal exercises do extend capability.

The practice of reflection that human life calls for, informed by sufficient reading and discussion with friends, is impossible without recognition of our inter-dependence. Hence, while we need to withdraw regularly into our own inner silence, that is likely to turn out to be unbearable unless we also make ourselves available as growing, sensitive listener-helpers who are prepared to walk alongside others' emotional tussles that often illuminate our own. Hence practicing serious personal emotional management demands endeavors to shape our lives within 'communities of love' that are everyday expressions of both practical and emotional support. Such communities may be specifically religious in affiliation. More often however they are simply experienced in the practice of family life, good neighboring and of mutual consideration in the varied contexts of employment and leisure.

There are no 'packages' to be transplanted in the area of emotional management. There are only hard-won precepts to follow. Principally these are space for reflection upon experience, listening through the 'inner ear', perceiving through the 'third eye', and holding the self in reasonable esteem with neither a debilitating guilt about failings around feelings, nor an unhealthy pride and self-satisfaction. If we seek integrity, we move, in a still relatively short life, perceptibly closer towards the reality of seeing both human and divine face to face. Unsurprisingly, this is often where our unconscious quest began as we struggled to find our face in the reflective countenance of at least one other, first our mother, then our father, or sister, brother or grandparent. Ponder the fact that babies do no know that they have faces!

Our journeys have commonalities amid many differences of detail. We share far, far more than difference, and can enter substantially into each-others emotions and consciousness. Unless we wish to hand over our lives to a totality of others' influence and wishes (beyond our control if we have severe dementia or stroke), our journey really is substantially in our hands, though there are never infinite degrees of freedom.

A new vision for a sustainable world, the living cosmos, has to come from two main sources The first of these is a popular mass commitment, through educational means, to *ecological rationality*, and this must include both its social and biophysical aspects. This means a devotion to reason enlightened by intuition and emotion. It is in stark contrast to the presently dominant ideology of materialism and economic determinism that we now know is likely to augur the terminal sickness of our species inside at most a handful of generations. Rational self-interest, espoused as the basis for free market economic exchange, is not now, if it ever was, an individual but a collective matter, a truly global issue.

The second aspect to feed fresh vision is the drive for personal integrity. This combines dimensions of ethics, emotion, reasoning and action. Hearts that beat to the call of considerate love and respect for others have their own forms of reasoning, not first driven by self-interest. Interplays of values, emotions and virtues enlighten the wisest ends to be pursued, a far wider canvass than means to achieve an end.

At the personal level, integrity must now become a quest for wholeness, even 'holiness', in spirit and in truth. Only that can endow contentment amid Earth's finite resources, which must become more widely shared so as to endow ecological sustainability. For me the quest for personal integrity, within the model of soul shown in diagram 13 , (page 239), has become a mosaic of light and shade, of giving up and holding on, of emotion with mind, of male with female, of bread with wine, of containing perplexity and paradox, of rooting hope, of faith that our oft hidden yet many-sided bereavements are and will remain bearable, and that there is an ever hiding yet abiding 'peace which passes all understanding'.

The desirable advances from the former and misplaced 'Enlightenment', as we should now call it, such as public health, human rights, material comforts, are not of themselves crucial because they do not address at depth the wounded, inner-perturbed human condition. Beyond basic survival, *we are not healed by material progress, but by redemption of the emotional mind, and re-attachment of the soul to its source and sense of destiny.* Integrity requires a sense of origins and destinies, just as a violin string is lost for sound unless secured by pivots at its ends. Good-enough parenting is the crucial foundation from origin; sound teaching its food, and mutuality its mechanism as we journey with a thereby sustainable individuality in the hope of leaving a wholesome legacy when our bodies decay.

Optimistically, in this global new millennium, we might edge with more confidence and conviction towards a new 'holistic enlightenment' grounded in a judicious synthesis of emotion, spirit, body and mind.

13.5 A codicil: poetry in e-motion

Rigorously trained in the sciences, I have in recent years been caught by surprise by the poetic idiom (see page v). Here I have used a few poetic lines, not as 'literature', but as summaries of some hard-won teaching. Poetic nuances can be suggestive and may help us to recognize important momentary symptoms of response, akin to 'a spirit passing before the face that makes the hair on our flesh stand up' (to paraphrase the Old Testament Book of Job 4:15).

Matthew Arnold (1822-88), scholar, poet and one of the UK's first schools' inspectors, predicted that without poetry, our science would appear incomplete. Genuine poetry does not appear through cleverness, whether 'trained' or of 'native wit', but from what my late friend scholar-poet Kathleen Raine called 'ancient springs'; trickles of truth resonating with our deepest nature. Arnold succinctly described poetry's character and function thus:

> 'Genuine poetry is conceived and composed in the soul. We turn to poetry to interpret life for us, to console us, to sustain us.'

Volume 2 of *Essays in Criticism*, 1888

William Wordsworth explicitly linked poetry to human emotion when he wrote:

> 'Poetry is the spontaneous overflow of powerful feelings; it takes its origin from emotion recollected in tranquility.'

Preface to Lyrical Ballads, 2nd edition, 1802

To suggest that you might develop your own emotional literacy and management partly through turning to quality poetry, which so often bridges emotion with the spiritualized intellect, enabling the dance between head and heart, would however be quite another story.

Below however, I attempt a summarising poem before a final review exercise.

Primal Emotions

Emotions pervasive,
Their control evasive;
Drivers of body, mind,
Mainly culture-blind.
May be sensory light,
Viewing world as bright;
Or weigh matter heavy,
Extracting painful levy
On human performing
Lacking spiritual forming.

Emotions may be long buried,
Their balance falsely steadied;
Yet none can be neatly excised
Nor character disguised,
And care over inner exploration
Eases soul transfiguration.

So finally I entreat you
To review your emotions
In your regular motions,
As you check your position,
Noting head-heart disposition;
For no one need be broken apart
Between hope, intellect and heart.

Beyond clouds of despair
Blue sky is ever there,
And calm is hope's best prayer
As grace for fears,
Or tears
In mind's eye;
So be wise far sooner than I.

© Richard Whitfield, 2005

Personal exercise 38 (a two-part review)

a) Early in the text (section 1.1, page 5) a list of 'probing questions' was given. Revisit those questions now in order to gain some sense of your growth in understanding. You might find that part (b) following is helpful within this review process.

b) This revision exercise contains 25 partly contrived word pairs in the order of the alphabet; only one letter, x, defying pairing, so prompting an alternative. For each letter eentry, note your associative thoughts and feelings prompted by the word pairs, involving some of the ideas in this book.

A. Anchor anger	N. Number numb
B. Block blame	O. Once overwhelmed
C. Connecting consciousness	P. Penetrating pain
D. Deadening depression	Q. Questions of quest
E. Esteeming essence	R. Reflectiveness revered
F. Faithing fear	S. Sordid shame
G. Ghastly grief	T. Timely touch
H. Hunger horror	U. Undercover umbrage
I. Irritating impulses	V. Vow void
J. Joined-up joy	W. Wound and wonder
K. Kindly kiss	X marks the spot where
L. Lost love	Y. Your youth
M. Minding marriage	Z. Zany zone

APPENDIX

Summarising index of personal exercises

SELECT BIBLIOGRAPHY

'Everything that is worth doing is the result of several minds playing on each other.'
Gustav Holst, composer, in the year of his death, 1934

Abbs P, *Against the Flow: Education, the Arts and Postmodern Culture*, Routledge, 2003
Bick D, *Counselling and Spiritual Direction*, Pentland Press, 1997
Birch C, *Feelings*, University of New South Wales Press, 1995
Bowlby J, *A Secure Base: Clinical Applications of Attachment Theory*, Routledge 1988.
Carter R, *Mapping the Mind*, Weidenfield and Nicholson, 1998
Coles R, *The Moral Intelligence of Children*, Bloomsbury, 1997
Cragg K, *Troubled by Truth: Life Studies in Interfaith Concern*, Pentland Press, 1992
Damasio AR, *Descartes' Error: Emotion, Reason and the Human Brain*, Putnam, 1994
Dixon, NF, *Our Own Worst Enemy*, Jonathan Cape, 1987
Dominian J, *Passionate and Compassionate Love*, Darton, Longman & Todd, 1991
Evans D, *Emotion: The Science of Sentiment*, Oxford UP, 2001
Goleman D, *Emotional Intelligence*, Bantam, 1995.
Kraemer S & Roberts J (eds), *The Politics of Attachment: Towards a Secure Society*, Free Association Books, 1996.
Handy C, *The Hungry Spirit*, Hutchinson, 1997
Hay D with Nye R, *The Spirit of the Child*, Fount, 1998
Hillman J, *The Force of Character and the Lasting Life*, Ballantine, 1999
Hoare CH, *Erickson on Development in Adulthood*, Oxford UP, 2002
Frijda NH, *The Emotions*, Cambridge UP, 1986
Frankl V, *Man's Search for Meaning*, Simon & Schuster, 1984
Gottman J, *Why Marriages Succeed or Fail*, Bloomsbury, 1997
Greenfield SA, *The Private Life of the Brain*, Penguin, 2000
Hurnscot L, *A Prison, A Paradise*, Gollancz, 1958
Jeeves M, *Mind Fields: Reflections on the Science of Mind and Brain*, Lancer/Apollos, 1994
Johnson RA, *The Psychology of Romantic Love*, Arkana 1987, and *Balancing Heaven and Earth*, Harper, 1998
Lake F, *Clinical Theology: A Theological and Psychological Basis to Clinical Pastoral Care*, (abridged by Yeomans M),
  and *In the Spirit of Truth: A reader in the work of Frank Lake* (ed. Carol Christian), Darton, Longman
  & Todd, 1986 and 1991
LeDoux J, *The Emotional Brain*, Weidenfield & Nicholson, 1998
Midgley M, *Beast and Man: The Roots of Human Nature*, Routledge, 2002
Miller A, *Timebends: A Life*, Methuen, 1987
Oatley K & Jenkins JM, *Understanding Emotions*, Blackwell, 1996
O'Donohue J, *Anam Cara: Spiritual Wisdom from the Celtic World*, Bantam, 1997
Olson DH &AK, *Empowering Couples: Building on Your Strengths*, Life Innovations, 2000
Parkes CM, Stevenson-Hinde J, & Marris P (eds), *Attachment Across the Life Cycle*, Routledge, 1991
Pearce JC, *The Biology of Transcendence: A Blueprint of the Human Spirit*, Park Street, 2002
E Rayner, *Human Development*, Routledge, 1993
Redfield J and Adrienne C, *The Celestine Prophecy: An Experiential Guide*, Bantam, 1995
Sachs J, *Faith in the Future*, Darton, Longman & Todd, 1995
Scott Peck, M, *Further Along the Road Less Travelled*, Simon and Schuster, 1993
Seligman M, *Authentic Happiness*, Nicholas Brealey, 2003
Sheldrake R & Fox M, *Natural Grace: Dialogues on Science and Spirituality*, Bloomsbury, 1996
Smith A, *The Theory of Moral Sentiments*, 1759 (Liberty Fund edition, 1984)
Spretnak C, *States of Grace: The Recovery of Meaning in the Postmodern Age*, Harper, 1991
Steiner G, *Real Presences: Is there anything in what we say?*, Faber , 1991
Toynbee P, *Part of a Journey*, Collins 1981, and *End of a Journey*, Bloomsbury, 1989
Waldron R, *Thomas Merton in Search of his Soul: A Jungian Perspective*, Ave Maria, 1994
Whybrow PC. *A Mood Apart: A Thinker's Guide to Emotion and its Disorder*, Picador, 1998
Winnicott DW, (edited essays) *Home is Where we Start From* Penguin, 1990
Wolpert L, *Malignant Sadness: The Anatomy of Depression*, Faber 1999.